MW01489877

MY *CURIOUS* LIFE

In Search of Love, Compassion, Authenticity, and Redemption

ANDREW SELIG

with Goody Lindley

This book is dedicated to many more people who have influenced me and my life than I can list here. Core among them are: Ellen, my wife, partner and best friend for over 50 years, without whom my life and efforts to continually understand and improve myself would be wanting. Sara and Becky, my extraordinary daughters, from whom I've learned more than they will ever realize, and who give me immense pride. My parents, who provided an incredible and indelible foundation of values, perspective, and love, and my grandparents and great grandparents, from whom I learned ways to live life explicitly and implicitly.

TABLE OF CONTENTS

FORWARD

If it weren't for my daughter, Sara, and granddaughter, Giuliana, this memoir would never have been written. I'd always thought that writing one's life story was a sign of ego, or only done by people with a remarkable story to tell, but one day, Sara said, "Dad, you really should write a memoir. If someone in your past had written one, think what it would have meant to you!"

Where I had been ambivalent when she had mentioned it in the past, I was finally swayed to saying yes. Our relationship had been somewhat challenging in the past, yet she wanted me to do this despite her disappointments in me and her sense that over the years I hadn't adequately recognized her feelings.

I can only hope that this book will bring us closer, deepen our understanding, and heal some wounds.

Giuliana was the tipping point. At age ten, she makes unusually astute observations about people and relationships, and asks intriguing questions – perhaps some of the answers she's looking for will be in these pages. There may be others too, perhaps in generations yet to come, who will be interested in and curious about their ancestors. As

Sara so astutely observed, I would have been delighted and gratified if one of my ancestors had left behind a story like this.

We all have a story that is unique and fascinating. We can learn so much from people's narratives that we can apply to our own lives. I hope mine meets this criterion.

I hope to be utterly honest and vulnerable in this book. Perhaps it will help me further understand the contradictions and inconsistencies I see in myself. To the extent that I know who I am, I want to show my authentic self. I want to acknowledge that others who read this and know me may, understandably, have different views of people and events that I describe from my perspective. We all perceive our outer world in the context of our inner world.

PROLOGUE

I don't have a lot of early memories. One that I do recall is playing with toy fire engines on the tiled hallway floor behind the heavy, old wooden door of the house on Dahlia Street in Denver that my parents' had recently purchased. I was probably four or five, anticipating the arrival of my paternal grandmother from St. Louis.

My parents had been living in Salt Lake City for about seven weeks. Shortly after I was born, on June 10, 1943, my dad, who was thirty-four, received a draft notice from the army. But ever since he'd seen his uncle in his dress blues, he had wanted to be a Marine. In his mind, the Marine Corps was an elite outfit, and if he had to fight for his country, he wanted the best training he could get – and that was with the Marines. He joined without telling my mom. She was furious, probably not fully grasping that he would be drafted anyway. So, in August of that year, she moved back to Denver to live with my maternal grandparents in a Denver Square, officially baptized an American Foursquare by the *Old House Journal* years later. As the name Foursquare implies, It was a square-shaped, two-story house with a big front porch and a little window peeking out from the center of a pyramid-shaped roof. A hallway ran through the center and a veranda graced the front, punctuated by a centrally placed door. These houses were popular in the city because they were easy to build and fit nicely into a small city lot. That house is now part of a historic block.

Another distant memory: opening the laundry chute door and yelling, "Woo! Woo!" Woo being the housekeeper's name. I also have a blurred memory melding into what I was told, of standing in my crib, pulling off my diaper, and smearing handfuls of feces on the wall, then drawing patterns with my pudgy fingertips. My grandfather, who generally wore a serious expression, walked into the room, and started laughing so hard he could barely breathe.

A clearer memory is of a live-in maid/nanny named Carrie, who I called Yingi. She had helped raise my mother and my mother's two younger fraternal twin siblings. After my dad joined the Marine Corps in 1943, and my mom and I moved back to my grandparents' house, Carrie said she wanted nothing to do with raising another child. However, she and I became quite attached, and I still have the crocheted throw blanket she made for me. Whenever Ellen or I or our daughters have been sick over the years, it has provided a warm hug of comfort.

Because I was the first grandchild in the family, I became the center of attention. My mom, aunt, grandmother, grandfather, and the nanny doted on me. I was their little prince. But about two years after enlisting, my dad came back from the service and we moved into a house of our own. And then my sister was born. I was instantly demoted from king to serf – at least that's how it must have felt. I'd been the sun everyone revolved around. Suddenly I was drifting aimlessly in a dark, cold void.

On my dresser today is a framed photograph of me at age three or four, sitting on the stairs of my grandparents' house. My expression is one of deep sadness. I've been looking at that photo for fifteen years, and I can occasionally go back to that feeling.

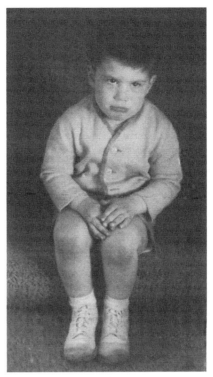

Figure 1My dresser picture

I was an emotional boy – and I'm an emotional man. Today, I'm profoundly in touch with my feelings. I cry readily and can attribute some of my sadness to missing my dad and my son-in-law both of whom I had loved dearly, but there's more than that. I believe there is a well of sadness inside me I have not yet fully explored. My tears are also related to feeling deeply moved by examples of human suffering and the making or breaking of strong human connections. The feeling is powerful, often rising to the surface when I'm alone.

I was an aggressive and adventurous kid, especially after my sister's birth, always getting into trouble of one sort or another, even getting expelled from every pre-school in the city. With nowhere else to turn, my parents took me to a psychiatrist. During one session at his office, I put a doll in a crib, picked up a bow and arrow, and shot the arrow straight into the doll's body. It doesn't take a lot of imagination or training to understand the symbolism.

The doctor wisely recommended enrolling me in Little League football and baseball to channel my energy into more productive pursuits.

A clear memory: my mother driving me in her 1950 Plymouth convertible to the park for my first practice. I may have been a bully, but I was so scared I sunk down in the back seat, hoping to make myself invisible. Sure, I could intimidate others, perhaps hoping they would never find out how easily I could be intimidated, but here I was, one of a group of kids my age, on a team with them! Bullying wasn't going to work here.

For years now, I have asked myself the questions: "What makes me tick? What is at the root of my emotions? Why am I the way I am?"

These are universal questions – and also deeply personal.

I've accomplished a great deal in my life and I'm proud of those achievements. I have immense drive. I don't give up easily. I've known success. At the same time, I have regrets. I've made mistakes. There have been times when I have not been the best me I could be, and I want to know why. What drove me to do the things I did? Why was I impatient with my children and with Ellen, my wife? What made me quick to anger? Will I ever understand? Will I ever have sufficient answers to these questions?

I don't know, but I'll never give up the search.

CHAPTER 1

ANCESTORS

My maternal grandmother was born Aimee Levi; my grandfather was Adolf Mayer. When I was ten, I interviewed my grandfather, wanting to know about his background. The story I wrote about him was later featured in a book titled, *Colorado Families: A Territorial Heritage,* compiled and published by The Colorado Genealogical Society in 1981.

Adolf was born in 1876 in the small town of San Luis, the oldest in Colorado. He was supposedly the first Anglo American born in a town of Hispanics. Soon after his birth, the family moved to Saguache where he grew up. Adolf's father, my great-grandfather, Leopold Mayer, who had emigrated from Alsace-Lorraine in the 1840s, walked beside his ox-cart in 1859 from Leavenworth, Kansas to Denver where he sat on the second city council. He then moved to Saguache where he started a bank and owned a general merchandise store.

Born in 1876, Adolf was the oldest of four boys. When he was fourteen or fifteen, his mother, Barbara Solomon Mayer, died, a fact that has brought tears to my eyes. I know how lost and sad he must have felt riding with the casket in the horse-drawn cart through the shivering cold to the railway station in Villa Grove. There, the train would take her body back to Denver for burial. How was he going to live without his mother?

Like me, I think his sadness found expression in anger because his father sent him to Notre Dame, a military prep school, to learn structure and discipline. He returned home after a year and eventually became a success in the furniture business. He retired at age forty and began lending money to start-up businesses.

Adolf was involved in the community, although at the time, society was openly prejudiced against Jews. Jewish doctors couldn't get appointments in hospitals and many clubs would not accept Jews. As a result, they set up their own organizations, hospitals, and clubs. My grandfather was one of several men who bought land to establish the Green Gables Country Club. Interestingly, Adolf withdrew from the club years later, probably because he and his wife deemed it too exclusive.

My maternal grandmother, Aimee, was born in Paducah, Kentucky, in 1888, one of four siblings including Edith, who I was fond of, and two boys that no one in the family talked about. I've always been curious about who they were and what they did that caused them to disappear. Aimee was ahead of her times. In a world where women rarely worked, she traveled to raise money for various organizations. At one point, she taught cooking at the Colorado Woman's College in Denver, and for years she was on the Board of The Denver Children's Hospital. YiYi, the name I called her, was outgoing, fun, and loving. I remember her telling me what a good man my dad was, and how important it is to be kind and loving to others.

I grew up aware of my family's conflicted feelings about their Jewish identity. My mother wasn't eager to be identified as Jewish. My parents believed that what you do and how you treat people are more important than whether you go to temple on Friday night and observe all the rituals.

Our family was secular as well as ambivalent. We belonged to the Reform Jewish Temple, but my parents left and started a separate synagogue along with some other families because they objected to their children marching around the temple waving Israeli flags. As far as they were concerned, we were Americans, and that was the primary way we should identify ourselves. I was also in the Young America Football league, with practices on Saturdays, which they deemed more important than Hebrew school.

They contributed ten thousand dollars to the new temple – an enormous sum of money in the 1950s, especially for a family that wasn't wealthy. That donation demonstrated the importance of Judaism in their lives, and yet we never celebrated Passover at our house. I went to Sunday School and I was confirmed, but my parents didn't regularly attend services and I did not have a Bar Mitzvah.

My mother, Emily, was particularly ambivalent. I think she believed that being Jewish held her back. In her college applications, she discovered that many had quotas for Jews. However, she did attend Skidmore in New York for two years. When my sister married a non-Jew and later divorced him, my mother told me that she urged her to retain her married name of Justice, which she thought sounded less Jewish. When my father came back from his service and they started looking for a place to live, they encountered signs in front windows that read *No Jews or dogs allowed.*

My mother was the oldest of three siblings – her younger brother, Adolf Jr. and sister, Barbara, were fraternal twins born in February 1919, two-and-a half years after her own birth. She felt displaced by them – a perfect echo of how I felt when my sister, Mary, was born. They had red hair and her entire life, my mother loved people with red hair. After the birth of the twins, my mom grew close to her grandmother, Emma Uri Levi Bernheim, who gave her some of the special attention she craved.

I think some of her alienation also manifested as anger when she was young. She told of the time she grabbed one of the twins by the ankles and swung them around until their head hit the radiator. No one who knew her as an adult would suspect her of such an act, or that she could be angry or mean in any way. She was kind, sweet, and gracious. Some people called her a "true lady," which I think she liked, but she also didn't want the label to explain who she was. Once, she was waiting for a parking place and another woman pulled in and took the space. My mom drove home, got an egg, and drove back to the parking lot where she broke it on the woman's windshield. I think there was a well of emotion boiling under the surface that she never showed.

I knew her as a person who fought for the underdog, maybe because she identified with them. And perhaps that was how she viewed my sister. I never doubted my mother loved me, but when she looked at me, she saw a son who she thought was good looking, had friends, and was athletic, so he didn't need much else. Mary got our mother's attention in a way I never did, but in a way I needed and wanted. My mother didn't and possibly couldn't, see how I struggled in school and how humiliating it was to be among the last chosen in front of the entire class in events like spelling bees.

In my view, Mary was mom's underdog, partly because she had learning disabilities. I think my mother understood how Mary felt, and even identified strongly with her emotions.

My father, Leon, wasn't as conflicted about Judaism as my mother. He could roll with the punches and keep his eye on the prize. Like me, he didn't believe in a god, but he still contributed his time and monetary resources to the new temple. But then, Judaism isn't entirely about religion – it's a diaspora that is largely cultural as well as religious. My wife, Ellen, and I have had the discussion many times: what is a Jew?

My answer to that is that a Jewish person is one who lives the values of Judaism. Ellen agrees, but also argues that this doesn't differentiate a Jew from someone who lives the values of any other religion. If Judaism as a religion is going to be perpetuated, some of the traditions should be celebrated. Still, I've always been unsure about my answer, and that's probably due to my upbringing. I've also thought the world might be a better place if somehow, magically, we could eliminate religions, since so much conflict and killing has been conducted in its name.

I had a very different relationship with my paternal than my maternal grandparents. My grandmother, Flossie, was born in 1881, and lived in St, Louis where my dad grew up. She'd divorced my grandfather, Mort, when dad was about fifteen. Mort moved to Florida and I never met him.

We would go to St. Louis a couple of times a year to visit my grandmother and she would come out to Denver perhaps twice a year. She told me a bit about her family – that she was the youngest of nine and her father was a mining engineer. She had a great sense of family, and I think that contributed to piquing my interest in my origins.

She had a little antique chair that had more sentimental value to her than monetary. The seat was made of wicker and she worried a great deal that someone would sit on the chair and break it. For her sake, I began to be concerned too and would tell people when they visited to be careful when they sat on the chair. Years later, in her will, she stated that she wanted me to have the chair. I value it a great deal – and, like her, not for monetary reasons.

She was a woman who had a clear sense of the right and wrong way to do things. My dad had that same internal structure. She didn't have much money, although her older siblings were business people in St. Louis who lacked for nothing. One was the head of a power company and another was an executive in a business that developed railway switches. She struggled after the divorce but she hadn't had an easy time of it before either. I understood she left Mort because he couldn't support the family, so the effort to make ends meet wasn't new to her.

My father described his dad as a nice guy, good with his hands, but also a hypochondriac (although he didn't use that word), who couldn't earn a lot of money because he had heart problems. He was probably the reason my father decided early on that he was going to earn a good living while never complaining about physical pain or discomfort.

I came to know my grandfather through some letters he wrote. Even thinking about them brings tears. He wrote to my dad and dad's older brother, Bill. They were simple letters. "How are you? How is Andy? How is Mary? I would love to hear from you. Please write."

It was the please in the last two words that opened my heart. But dad must have been too angry and disappointed to respond. I wondered, was Mort like me? Was he just a sensitive man who desperately wanted contact with his kids? But they were so angry with him. It was the please – the pleads that touched me – how it must have hurt his heart to be cut off from the children he loved.

My dad died at age ninety-five. In all those years, I only saw him cry once, when I was about fifteen and we were in Salt Lake City and he heard that his father had died.

Over the years, I asked him, "Why didn't you ever respond to your dad?"

I never got an answer I understood. I don't even remember what he said – all I know is he wept when his father died.

Mort was the oldest of five boys. Today I'm in contact with some of my cousins, but no one knew Mort well. Even though I never met him, I feel a certain kinship with this man who was clearly sensitive and wanted a deeper connection that was ultimately denied him.

CHAPTER 2

CHILDHOOD

Looking back, I find it difficult and complex to evaluate my childhood. In some ways it was a happy and satisfying one, and in other ways less so. I believe my unhappiness was buried so deep I didn't recognize it. Looking back now, it's easier to see.

Most of my memories are good ones that include playing Little League football and baseball. I was a good athlete and sports made me feel special while also giving me an avenue to channel my aggressiveness and make friends.

Figure 2 I'm holding the football...city champs.

I recall spending hours playing hide and seek and "cowboys and Indians." While most of the kids wanted to be cowboys, I was always more interested in the part of the Indians, specifically Geronimo.

I was intensely curious about how things work, but in my quest to understand, I rarely thought about consequences. One time, I wanted to know how a lock worked, so I took apart the back door knob while my dad was out of town on a business trip. My mom was understandably upset, especially when I had trouble figuring out how to put it back together.

I have an early memory of my dad coming into my room, waking me up, and saying, "Get dressed fast! There's a two-alarm alarm fire!" He remembered going to a fire house near where he lived in NYC when he was young and I think the experience ignited a lifetime interest in firemen and fighting fires. My parents listened to fire and police calls on a radio for years and would drive around on a weekend evening listening and going to some of the calls. Occasionally, my sister and I came along. Years later, chasing police calls became something I loved to do, and I only stopped when the police went to radios that civilians couldn't listen to.

From the time I was very young until my early adolescence, we had dinner at my grandparent's house every Sunday. My grandmother had a terrific sense of humor while my grandfather was quiet and more serious, but he had a certain presence about him. Sitting at the head of the table after dinner, he would pull out his pocket knife and deftly carve an apple into eight or sixteen pieces for dessert.

I remember walking by his bedroom one night, the only illumination coming from a distant light. Through the open door, I saw him, a shadowy figure on the floor, doing push-ups on his fingertips. The sight must have made an indelible impression because I have done push-ups on my fingertips all my life until my wrists and thumbs no longer allowed it. But I still do push-ups now on my hands.

But I don't think I was only emulating the action I saw; I think I wanted to be more like him. He was as much a hero to me as any of the cowboy legends of the Old West.

Memories like this bring up deep emotions. I see and experience them as clearly as if they happened yesterday, and I want to go back and connect with the people and the time.

I recall one special day when I was ten or twelve, trekking down the steep basement stairs of my grandparent's house with my mother and grandfather. Up against one of the cold cement walls was a cedar trunk. He opened the heavy lid, lifting out a .22 Colt rifle, a rare item from a manufacturer known for its pistols. It had been his as a boy, and it was still in perfect condition when he gave it to me.

Then he presented me with something even more valuable: a Navajo weaving, known as a Chief's blanket. One of the most iconic weavings in American history, Navajo Chief Blankets were a distinguished status symbol during the 19th century that were traded and prized throughout the Southwest and Great Plains. The phase one, two, and three blankets were often worn across the shoulders of a Chief, clan leader, or men and women of prominent social or financial status. My weaving was a phase two, a style that made each blanket stand out with more vivid color and style that the previous phase. My great grandfather had probably acquired it when he was in the mercantile business in Saguache.

I still have the weaving. About ten or fifteen years ago, I brought it to an expert in Navajo weavings who was visiting a museum in Denver. I handed him a few items in a bag, with the chief's blanket at the bottom. The expert pulled out the items one by one, about fifty people gathered around. He was appreciative of the items I'd brought, identifying each one quickly, accurately, and professionally. Lastly, he pulled out the chief's blanket and gasped. "Oh f**k! Do you know what you have here?"

I did. And I was inordinately pleased by his reaction.

For a while, I hung it on a wall, but then took it down, for fear of moth damage. It is now a treasured item rolled up safely in my grandfather's cedar trunk. And to think that he had slept under it when he was growing up. It was just a blanket on his bed that kept him warm.

Another memory that stands out is of my mother lying in bed because of her migraine headaches. She didn't complain about them; she would just say she had a headache, walk into her bedroom, turn off the lights, put opera music on the radio, and drape a cold washcloth on her forehead. I aways felt bad for her because I knew the pain was debilitating and there was nothing I could do. There were times, especially when I was very young, that I worried she would die. When I was older, I asked what I could do and she would let me push my fingers hard into the base of her head, giving her some temporary relief.

More meaningful memories include making and flying model airplanes, building a go-kart with a lawnmower engine, summers as a day camper and then a junior counselor, sitting on my dad's shoulders to watch parades, and target practice with my dad. We would go to the mountains with my parents and sister, cook over an open fire, and eat hamburgers and potatoes cooked with bacon. I also remember watching trains go by at the railroad station in Denver, visiting with my grandparents, especially Boppa and Yiyi, my mother's parents, and sitting in the back seat while my dad drove in the mountains with the top down, the wind in my face, looking for hawks and eagles soaring in the sky or perched high on utility poles. There were track and field days in elementary school and junior high, playing "bombardment" in my elementary school gym, and getting out of bed when my parents had company and sneaking into the dining room to hear the grown-ups talk. We visited H-G ranch in Estes Park where I rode horses and explored the area around the ranch, talking with the wranglers. I recall going to Lakeside amusement park with friends on my birthdays, tagging along with my neighbor,

Frank Metzger, when he delivered newspapers, accompanying him to University of Denver hockey games, and listening to 1940s and 50s songs on a windup record player.

Frank was the older brother I always wanted. Being the special cool guy he was, I admired his sense of style: Levi jeans without a belt and white socks with his penny loafers. To this day I wear Levi jeans, white socks, and sometimes, no belt.

Our parents took us out for dinner every Thursday night at a diner or an inexpensive restaurant. We were never lavish – we drank only water and never ordered dessert, but it was still a treat. Eating dinner together was one of the "rules" at our house. We almost always had interesting discussions about world affairs, the volunteer work my parents were doing, equality, ethics, and political issues of the day.

Family dinner wasn't the only rule at our house. My dad was strict and had explicit expectations. Mary and I had to leave the house or come in by the back door; we didn't use the living room unless we had company; we were not allowed to put our feet up on the furniture; we were supposed to step on the walks, not on the grass; we were expected to say please and thank you and to stand up when someone entered the room, especially if they were older; if we wanted to leave the table, we had to ask to be excused – and we might not be; we could pile as much food on our plates as we wanted, but we were expected to eat it all, and if we didn't, we could anticipate sitting there for a very long time until we did; if we wanted to play catch or kick-ball, we had to go to the park at the corner – not the backyard; cabinet doors and drawers should be closed and opened softly – never banged; when we left the house we had to close the doors softly – never slammed shut, especially not the screen door at the back on a tightly-coiled metal spring; I had to put things away immediately after using them, and everything had its proper place. My clothes and gear belonged in my room, and my room had better be tidy. Tools had to be kept oiled and in good condition.

My dad may have been strict, but he also knew how to have fun. So did my mother. One night, my dad was sitting at the dinner table and he said something to my mother that was pretty critical. She picked up the bowl of mashed potatoes and gravy and upended it over my dad's bald head. I have a photo of him hanging over the sink, his mouth split open in a huge grin, doing his best to wipe the mess off his scalp. My mother is standing in the background, her hand covering her mouth, her body obviously shaking in laughter.

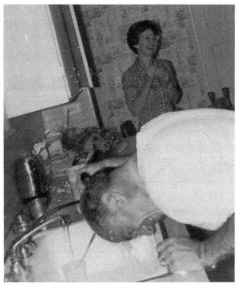

Figure 3 My mom feeling so satisfied responding to my dad's being critical

Probably because there were four years between us, Mary and I didn't have a lot in common and didn't play together. In many ways, I wasn't particularly nice to her. But we had our moments. I must have been twelve or thirteen when she wrote me a note apologizing for getting me into trouble. Generally, I deserved all the trouble that came my way for the pranks I pulled on her. Her note read, "Andy, I'm so sorry I got you into trouble, but I didn't think dad would get as mad at you as he got."

Figure 4 My dad, myself, Mary and my mother late 1950's

My parents frequently excused me from the dinner table for a number of reasons like bad manners or talking back to them. I'd have to leave and go to my room, often still pretty hungry. My dad would then allow me a piece of bread sprinkled with seasoned salt. One time, when I'd been sent to my room because I'd poked Mary, and she'd screamed in exaggeration of the pain, she slid a piece of bread with seasoned salt under the door of my room.

I came home with terrible report cards – and not just the grades. The comments ran the gamut from, "Andy needs to focus" and "Andy needs to behave better" to "Andy must listen and follow directions better" and "Andy talks too much in class."

My biggest anxiety and concern in school was spelling – and I still can't spell well. We had spelling tests on Fridays and both parents – mostly my dad – would go over the words with me on Thursday nights. Despite their best efforts, I just couldn't get it. It was frustrating for me, and I'm sure equally so for my dad. But he was endlessly patient with all the subjects, including math, another subject I struggled with.

I had two aunts who meant a lot to me: my mother's sister, Bobbi, who I called Aunt Bobbin, and Aunt Eileen who was married to Uncle Adolf. Aunt Bobbin was fun and artistic, and best of all, she thought I was terrific. Eileen also built me up. Whenever she gave me a small gift, she'd include a card with messages that meant a great deal to me, telling me I was special – and why I was special.

I think we need people like that in our lives – people who build us up, see our better sides, and encourage us to be and do our best. I particularly needed them because my dad was tough and I wanted more recognition, love, and tenderness from him – and from my mother. Having it from my aunts meant a lot.

The Children of Kauai was a study that examined children who grew up in extreme poverty on the Hawaiian island of Kauai, and while most turned into dysfunctional adults, about a third became exemplary members of society. The difference? Those who succeeded had had a mentor – a coach, a teacher, or a neighbor who had taken an interest in them and supported them. Certainly, I didn't come from that sort of environment, but I was lucky to have people in my life who encouraged me and who cared.

CHAPTER 3

DAD AND MOTHER

I did some wild and dangerous things in junior high school, and even later, constantly craving excitement, trying to create a certain persona, and testing limits with my parents, teachers, and strangers. I liked to set up situations where I did something challenging and fun and could then observe how others reacted, and later, try to wriggle out of the consequences. Some of my motivation stemmed from a desire to get the attention I wanted from my parents. But they knew nothing about some of my misadventures – not until I told them years later. I was also motivated by trying to prove to myself I could do something that I feared was beyond me.

I still get an adrenaline rush from doing and saying challenging things. I think I have an appetite for being provocative and testing myself. Today, however, my actions are less dangerous and rarely at other people's expense.

In addition to testing limits and taking chances, I wanted my dad's approval. I thought he was tough on me, but I was also making it hard for him to give me the recognition I craved. I used his supposed toughness to explain some of my more roguish behavior. I told myself I was rebelling against my dad. I wanted to be my own person. At the same time, I wanted him to show his love in ways I would recognize.

My father thought of himself as a matter-of-fact guy. On more than one occasion he told me not to get too excited about life's highs and not to get too down about the lows. His words echoed the Buddhist concept of noticing the feelings, acknowledging them, and then re-engaging in the present. He seemed to have mastered the art, but I wanted him to be less matter-of-fact and more empathetic to my feelings. Perhaps what I called "tough" was partly his stoicism.

In my eyes, enrolling in the Marines in 1943 took a tremendous amount of courage. I've often wondered, could I have done that? I don't know, but I don't think so. Am I that brave? Probably not. He stepped forward, knowing his decision would very likely put him on the front lines. I fear I would likely have been with the majority. I've wondered if some of my motivation to get into fights was to try to prove to myself that I, too, was tough and had the courage I so admired in my dad.

When I think of my dad, the first word that comes to mind is courage, but he had many more admirable qualities. He was a hard worker and strove to be financially independent. He had friends and family who were successful in business, and he wanted to match them, but only through his own efforts.

My dad looked up to and wanted to emulate his maternal grandfather, William Einstein, who was born in Frankfurt on Main, Germany, and immigrated to the US after marrying Sophie Rothchild in 1853. He was a successful mining engineer and a principle in starting the Texas Gulf Sulfur Mining Company. My dad admired his grandfather's work ethic, discipline, and focus on family. He told me about walking with him in New York City and being given a candy bar – clearly, a precious memory.

I believe my dad was tough to work with, hovering nearby while trades people did their jobs. I admit to having the same trait – I'll observe a worker closely, asking questions, wanting to learn what they are doing, and hopefully being sensitive to subtle messages to leave them alone to do their jobs. Like my dad, I've had success working with others in organizational settings, but most of my professional endeavors have been in my own practice with obligations only to my clients.

My father was demanding and he was a perfectionist, reluctant to give up on a project even when conventional wisdom said he should. He worked his way up in the May Department Store chain from stock boy in St. Louis to buyer and then assistant to the president in Denver. Later, he was a sales rep for various products, and went into real estate, buying a house, renovating, and selling at a profit. He even built a couple of apartment buildings – always on his own.

He was a perfectionist in other ways too. You could do anything one way – or you could do it the right way, and the right way was usually the way my dad thought it should be done.

I had chores, not to earn an allowance, but because I was a member of the family and I was expected to contribute. I swept the garage and the sidewalks, cut the grass, set the table, cleared the table, and helped with the dishes. To this day, my muscle memory guides some of my chores. While my wife, Ellen, does most of the cooking, I tend to do the cleaning up. When Ellen cooks, she uses all our counter space – and we have a lot of counter space. There are times when it's almost impossible to stop myself from cleaning up behind her, because I know I'm going to be tidying up after dinner and I really want to get a head start on it.

I can't count how many times Ellen has said, "Andy, I'm not through with that – don't put it away." Or, "Andy, where's the butter?"

"Oh, I'm sorry. I put it back in the refrigerator."

My dad was also committed to shaping the community to help people and align it with his values. He started as a volunteer at the Auraria Community Center serving young Hispanic men in a low-income area. In his thirty years with the center, he served as a board member and chair for more than a decade. I still feel proud of him when I recall that he was the only Anglo asked to remain on the Board of Directors during the turbulent sixties when the community wanted a Hispanic Board. He also worked for decades with Planned Parenthood, and was on the board at the state and national levels.

I wanted my kids to see me the way they saw my dad – their grandfather. They respected and admired him, and sought his advice. It hasn't been until quite recently, that they've given me some of that approbation. I wasn't my dad. I tried to be tough like him while also being in touch with my kids' thoughts and feelings, but where his toughness came from an authentic place of calmness and certainty, mine had an undercurrent of impatience and anger.

I believe I've been more influenced by my dad than my mom. They shared many values, but she was less explicit about them. My work ethic, my "never give up" attitude, my commitment to contributing to my community, standing up for what I believe in, and not compromising my values reflected him, although my mother surely passed on some of her own high standards. From my father I learned to set goals and do everything I could to achieve them – and I've done that in various ways in my professional pursuits and volunteer activities. I attribute a lot of my success to the lessons my dad passed on.

Later in his life, my dad tested positive for learning disabilities. My sister also tested positive, while I was borderline. Dad wasn't the intellectual my mother was and did not read for pleasure, but he studied company brochures and business briefs. He assiduously went over information about his real estate pursuits and investment portfolio. His broker still recalls how carefully my dad went over annual reports. He was an astute businessman.

My mother was an avid reader who also kept up on current events and new trends. She was the academic influence in my life. She also contributed to my motivation to volunteer and help others. I was enamored with Abraham Lincoln when I was young, and believed she was like him because of her concern for people and her contributions to the community as a volunteer. My dad gleaned information more organically. He had an insatiable curiosity about people. Meeting them for the first time, he'd ask questions: "What do you do? How do you do that? Why does it work that way?" He listened keenly to their answers, not to reply, but to learn. He was certainly as smart as my mother or anyone else I knew.

He told me, "It's important to learn about other people and to learn from them." His attitude and words have been a big influence on me and my career. I have felt challenged to ask good questions and to genuinely listen without anticipating or formulating what I am going to say next. It can lead to awkward pauses – but the conversation is authentic.

I may have wanted more attention from my dad, but the fact is, he showed that he cared about me. He came to all my Little League baseball and football games. He even attended a lot of practices. At one point, at age eleven or twelve, I was overweight by just a few pounds for my age group, so before weigh-in I soaked in a hot tub, sweating out water weight, then put on sweat pants and a sweat shirt and ran all the way to the weigh-in site with my father driving slowly beside me in his Plymouth convertible, keeping pace, silently cheering me on.

My negative behavior started early. I was in grade school, walking to school one day, and Joanne, a girl a few years older, was walking on the other side of the street. Without a thought for consequences, I picked up a rock, wondering if I could hit her with it. Then I took aim and threw it, catching her squarely on the temple.

I walked home, found my mother making the bed in her room, and said, "Mommy, I just did a terrible thing."

"Tears spilled out of her eyes. "Andy," she said, her voice immeasurably sad. "I just don't know what I'm going to do with you." I feel regret and shame to this day about what I did to the girl and the hurt I caused my parents.

Another time when I misbehaved, my mother was intent on spanking me. I got the dining room table between us and tore around it while she tried to catch me. She didn't stand a chance. While she grew more and more frustrated, I was crowing inside, delighted that I was faster and could stay out of her reach indefinitely.

Making my mother cry was almost worse than whatever it was I had done. And yet, I kept doing things I knew I shouldn't. Why? An adrenaline rush? More than that, I think. I felt some internal reward. Was it the challenge I imposed on myself? Was it that I was getting the attention I needed? Was it all about proving my autonomy – that normal rules of behavior didn't apply to me?

But I wasn't entirely bad. I tried to befriend kids who had no friends. I remember Johnny, who signed my grade school autograph book with, "To the nicest boy in the class." Maybe I identified with the misfits and those who were bullied. In that same grade school book, a sixth-grade teacher wrote "To Andy, who constantly displays the true meaning of sportsmanship." Those words have resonated with me ever since, and I try to constantly measure up to them.

A seminal event in my childhood occurred when I was only six. I was feeling left out, not getting the attention I needed. I had just enrolled in Little League, and Mike, at age sixteen, was my coach. He became my idol and, in many ways, my savior. He gave me the attention I so desperately craved. He called me "Lucky Life" because I was a good football and baseball player. I hit well and could catch almost anything, but I threw so badly, Mike once suggested I toss the ball underhand. But he built up my self-esteem. He was my sun and moon and stars. I wanted to make him proud.

My parents knew how I felt about Mike and invited him to join us at a dude ranch one summer where they got him his own cabin.

When I was ten, he invited me into his basement where he molested me. It happened a couple of times. It wasn't more than touching, but I didn't know how to feel. Weird? Yes. My parents had no idea. They were grateful that a young man was taking an interest in me, but my grandmother was suspicious. Why was a twenty-year-old man spending so much time with a young boy? The day I came home with a jock strap, my parents started asking questions. I don't remember exactly what I said, but I must have told them what had happened.

What is clear is how well my father handled the situation. I was lying on my back in my bed, my dad sitting at the foot of the bed, telling me that what Mike had done was wrong. It wasn't my fault.

My heart was in my stomach, less because of what Mike had done physically, but because of the betrayal. I'd wanted him to like me, approve of me, and care about me. Losing him felt like losing a big chunk of my world.

I wasn't ready for the proverbial "birds and bees" father-son talk, but my dad felt it best to explain it to me. When he told me about intercourse, I said, "How will I know what to do?"

"Don't worry," he said. "When the time comes, you'll know what to do."

If anything good came out of that incident, it was our secret joke. Every now and then over the years I would call my dad, even after I married Ellen, and say, "Okay, dad, the time has come. Now, tell me what to do!"

It turned out that one of my good friends, the football team's star quarterback, was also molested by Mike. When my dad found out, he called my friend's father, but he was adamant about not telling Mike's dad who was a strict Catholic with a reputation for being mean. Instead, the two men sent Mike for a psychiatric evaluation. The doctor labelled Mike's behavior as "aberrant adolescent experimentation." Today, that diagnosis would be highly questionable.

And the psychiatrist was wrong. Mike continued to molest young boys. When I was in graduate school working on my doctorate, I noticed his name in the newspaper and wrote a letter to his trial judge explaining my relationship to Mike and offering my help as a graduate student in psychology to the kids involved in the case. I never received a response.

Years later, I was sitting in a chair in a local barbershop when Mike's dad walked in. Sitting next to him, I heard him say to the barber, "Mike was wrongly accused of doing something to kids."

Do I say something? Should I? He's wrong! But he's Mike's dad! Is it right for me to tell him?

I could have said, "What he's accused of is what he did to me." But what good would it serve? Why destroy a father's image of his son? I heard a few years ago that Mike was murdered in prison.

CHAPTER 4

ENTREPRENEURSHIP AND TROUBLE

I experienced another significant event when I was ten. My dad encouraged me to sell Christmas wreaths and table decorations door-to-door. Such a simple undertaking, and yet it taught me the rudiments of business, gave me confidence in my ability to sell, and brought my dad and me closer together.

I bought samples from the local couple who made the decorations using money I'd saved from shining my father's shoes: twenty-five cents per shine and they had to be Marine Corps perfect! I went door-to-door with the samples, taking orders and following my dad's instructions on what to say and how to say it to get the sale. I would take the orders, buy the finished products, and deliver them to my customers. I made a fair amount of money that I saved on my father's advice. To this day, I believe it was a terrific experience that taught me a lot while also raising my self-confidence.

In high school, I sold Fuller brushes door-to-door and did well in that endeavor too. I encouraged sales by offering a small vial of men's cologne. Incredibly, I still have one of those samples. I also sold magazines, enticing housewives with a free sample of *Good*

Housekeeping. One weekend my magazine selling boss had to go out of town, and to reward me for my sales success, he let me use his 1960 fuel injected Corvette for the weekend. I had two days and nights of incredible fun.

I became a good salesperson, a skill I can never underestimate. We all have to do sales, whether it's selling magazines or convincing our kids of the value of cleaning their room. I've sold brushes and wreaths and my services as a psychologist. As tough as I think my dad was, I believe he managed to tread the fine line between being demanding and not destroying my confidence and self-esteem. Until a few months before he died, he never said he was proud of me, nor did he tell me when he thought I'd done well. He may have been afraid I'd stop striving to do better. However, he did tell other people he was proud of me, and when they told me that after he died, I was deeply gratified.

I probably had a genetic bent towards resiliency, but I can't underestimate my dad's influence. As a child, I often thought he was too much. From the wisdom gained over many years, I think he knew how much to push and when to ease up. He managed it well, and I am grateful he was my father.

Growing up, I was more afraid of my dad than the police, and I had a few run-ins with the latter. But when the cops brought me home, I was more afraid of disappointing my dad than of any punishment the law could hand out. He hit me on my rear with his belt about half a dozen times, a common disciplinary practice at the time, and even then, I suspect it was because neither of my parents knew what to do with me.

But those spankings weren't as dramatic as the word would imply. I usually knew it was coming and would stuff an extra pair of underwear or newspapers down my briefs. Of course my father knew, but he said nothing. He was likely happy I'd done it. And I wasn't afraid of those brief swats – I feared losing his love, attention, and approval.

I was eleven or twelve when I built a chug, or go-kart using an old lawnmower engine. I think I might actually have stolen the mower. I took the little three-horsepower engine apart and put it back together more than once, puttering in the garage for hours. I wanted to know how it worked. I tweaked it to make it more powerful, and then I added a long exhaust pipe to amplify the sound. To this day, I am enamored of the vroom vroom of a big V8 engine.

When my chug was ready, I put it on the street – no brakes – zooming along at about twenty mph. What an adrenaline rush! Until a motorcycle cop pulled me over. He got off his bike and strode over in his gleaming knee-high leather boots, looming over me like a human Godzilla. He brought me to my house where I rang the doorbell. My dad opened it. The officer gave him an accurate rundown about how fast I was going, the fact I had no brakes, and how stupidly dangerous it all was. My dad was not happy.

I was twelve when he bought me a single shot .22 rifle because he wanted me to know how to handle weapons safely and be responsible with them. I have wonderful memories of target practice with my dad, but another memory still pains me. When I was in junior high, I wanted to test how far a .22 bullet would travel. I was in my room with the clear thought, *I shouldn't do this.* But I wanted to know – what would this bullet do? I aimed at my bed and pulled the trigger. The bullet penetrated both mattresses, the floor beneath, and lodged in the basement.

My parents were furious. What I had done went against everything my father had taught me, and my mother hadn't even wanted a gun in the house.

I had another police encounter at age sixteen, driving in downtown Denver with friends, probably looking for trouble. Someone gave another driver the finger – it was probably me. The driver got out of his car, standing a whole lot taller than me, strode over to my open driver's side window and jabbed me solidly in the face. Somehow the police got involved, and pretty soon I was sitting in the police station with my dad, hearing the detective telling me, "Young man, if you go around looking for trouble, you're always going to find it. And you're always going to find someone bigger, stronger, and tougher than you."

He was right, and I knew he was right, but I was sixteen. I didn't listen.

A little bit of that sixteen-year-old still lives inside me, still responds to that adrenaline rush, and still wants to test limits.

More trouble: a friend had a car just like mine: a '53 Oldsmobile. I tuned it up for him in front of our house and jumped in for a test drive. I floored it, whipping down the street at close to sixty. At the end of the block, a woman was preparing to drive through the intersection, kids in the back seat. She pulled out, probably unaware of my speed in a twenty-mph zone. Too late to brake. She slammed into me. I hung on to the steering wheel and slid to my left where the door had swung open. A split second later, I smashed into a tree and slid over to the passenger seat – and all the time, kids screaming, filling my senses with terror.

Miraculously, no one was hurt, but those sounds, those feelings, the second-by-second details, are carved in my memory.

I knew the policeman who came to the scene as a friend to the local high school kids. After assessing the situation, he told me, "Andy, from now on, you are going thirty miles an hour." And then he gave the other driver a ticket.

My father would not have been so lenient. He ran down the street to the accident scene. "What happened?" he asked.

"I got into an accident and it was my fault," I said.

"No, really Andy – what happened?"

"That's what happened. I was going too fast and this woman pulled and hit me. She didn't know how fast I was going. It was at least partly my fault."

I don't remember his next words or actions, but the sense of his disappointment remains strong. I wanted him to approve of me and feel pride in me, but my need for excitement and thrills, and pushing the limits, sabotaged my better judgement too often. Many years later, in my sixties, my dad and I had a good laugh when I told him I no longer regretted proving myself in Marine Corps bootcamp, because he'd had me in it as my drill sergeant for sixty years!

About ten years ago, as a hospice volunteer, I came across the name of the policeman who had come to the accident scene. Was this the same Bob? It was. He was about ninety when I began spending time with him in the year before he died. I learned that he was a World War II veteran and hero. I listened to his stories with great interest and admiration. Before he died, he gifted me with a square he crocheted with the word *smile*. I remember him with great fondness whenever I look at it.

I find it difficult to reflect on the relationship with my dad: what I wanted, what I feel I got, and how it impacted me. On reflection, I'm grateful he was my father, and that I learned many invaluable lessons and values from him. He and Ellen have been the major influences in my life. I wanted more of my dad's acceptance and approval, but did I use his lack of praise as an excuse for some of my behavior – my lack of motivation?

I built high expectations for myself and then struggled to live up to them. As an adult, I came much closer to the mark, but as a boy, I disappointed myself. A stranger or distant acquaintance might be impressed with my education and professional accomplishments, and in fact, I have a good deal to be proud of. There are times I have a good sense of that, but at other times, I find myself focusing on what I could have or should have done better. I feel regret for a variety of things, many of them related to my wife and daughters, but others focusing on my childhood: not going farther with my scouting, harming other kids, and letting my parents down at times.

If I set a high bar for myself, I have to ask why. Most obviously, perhaps I was trying to emulate my dad who expected a lot of me and who was so courageous in my eyes. But am I too quick to credit my dad for the good I have done and also too quick to attribute my negative behaviors on his influence? It feels too glib and easy. But I so wanted his affirmations – his pats on the back.

The fact is, instead of working hard, I often took the easy way out, and maybe my dad saw that and that was reason enough for him to withhold his praise. But he hadn't received that sort of attention from his dad either. His own childhood experiences must have had a big influence on his ideas of being a good father. Judging from his letters and the few things my dad told me about his father, he was a lovely, sensitive man who couldn't hold down a job or support his family. My father was probably being the kind of dad he'd wanted for himself – a dad who was present and who set high standards and goals for his children.

I think some of my standards and motivation to do well also came from other family members, particularly my maternal grandfather who was a successful businessman, and two great-grandfathers who started with nothing and went on to live successful lives. They have certainly inspired me to do something meaningful with my own life.

CHAPTER 5

GROWING UP

I was twelve in 1955. It was a warm spring day – blue skies, maybe a few fat white clouds drifting lazily with the breeze, and bees buzzing in the rose bushes. I was riding my red Hawthorne bike down the street, the handlebars turned around to allow me to more easily reach the bags of newspapers I was delivering on my regular route. The thought suddenly came to me that I didn't want to get older.

I wish I could stay twelve and not deal with whatever is coming, because I'll have to deal with it, like it or not.

I wanted to stop my personal time-clock right there. I'd been leaving childhood behind for a while, becoming more aware of life's challenges, knowing that plans don't always work out, and eventually, everyone would die.

But no one can stop time.

I didn't like school. Classes were hard. My cohort were the intelligent capable kids, and when I compared myself to them, I didn't feel smart, nor did I measure up to them.

Sports were my saving grace. For several years, I was awarded five or six second place ribbons and one blue ribbon for first place in track and field events. With each second-place ribbon, I was behind my friend, Russ, and the first-place ribbon was awarded to our relay team that included Russ. He was a much better athlete than me, and no matter how hard I tried, I could not measure up to him.

Leaving my elementary school and entering junior high in seventh grade was a frightening experience. Fresh out of sixth grade – top of the totem pole – and tossed down to the bottom, we not only had to adjust to the new school, but we also endured the ritual of "smearing" that entailed being tracked down after school by the older kids and having our entire faces coated with lipstick. There was no escaping it.

In my life I've put on a good show of bravado on many occasions, looked for trouble, found it, gotten into fights, and managed to survive. But there's another part of me that has always been afraid of being beaten up. I believe I am counterphobic, which means I seek out situations I fear in an attempt to overcome the dread or prove to myself I'm not afraid.

I had a reputation for being rough and tough, but underneath the façade, I didn't feel all that dangerous. Still, I kept up the image and continued to do things that strengthened it. I was about ten or eleven, standing on the walk outside our house one day when the paperboy came by. He was older and bigger than me and I should have known better, but for no other reason than I felt like it, I threw a snowball at him, catching him squarely on the chest.

He braked, jumped off his bike and came at me too fast for me to react. He threw me down and started punching my face hard. Through the shock and pain, I could still see my parents standing by the front door, watching. My mother told me later that she wanted to intervene but my dad said, "No. Andy asked for it and he's got to deal with the consequences."

I'd like to believe it taught me a lesson, and maybe it did, but it didn't stop me from testing the limits. I just got better at avoiding consequences.

I was a bit older when I was shooting baskets at the hoops court at the end of our block. Two or three guys, a couple of years older than me and definitely bigger came onto the court with their ball and pushed me away.

"Hey!" I said, "I was here first!"

They shrugged and played. I may as well have been a pesky gnat to be brushed aside and ignored.

I felt the humiliation and rage building in my chest. Then, I grabbed their ball and either threw or kicked it away. That got their attention. One of the guys laid into me – a beating so bad, he broke my nose.

I scrambled away and tore home holding my hand under my nose to catch the blood. I slammed through the back door and dashed past my parents, shouting, "I'm getting my gun! I'm going to kill him!"

I don't know what I would have done if my dad hadn't stopped me. I was blind with anger, shame, helplessness, and a torrent of unnameable emotions.

It would have been so easy to just let them have the hoops court and walk away. But I couldn't. I didn't want to give in because pushing me off wasn't right. Maybe my penchant for testing limits and pushing boundaries wasn't always about looking for trouble. Sometimes, it was about justice.

Today, some of that kid on the basketball court still lives inside me. There are many times in my life when I have not taken the smart or easy way out. I will still defend myself. I will still not be pushed around. You are not going to humiliate me. That attitude has gotten me into trouble more than once. Thankfully, Ellen has been a great balance to my impulsiveness, helping me think things through and weigh the consequences.

In junior high, I began to like a few of my classes: gym, because I was a good athlete, and science, because I liked the concept of the subject. I was particularly interested in biology and how the body works. I would have liked to have gone into medicine and become a physician, but my ability to retain and regurgitate facts and details wasn't good enough. I also didn't develop the study and work ethic early enough to pursue a science track.

My memories of junior high are not especially good ones. I was inevitably the last person chosen in class when we had a spelling bee. Or I would stand at the board attempting to diagram a sentence, without a clue about the process. I didn't know how to study and I didn't apply myself, largely because I didn't think I could.

I acted out and, as a result, found myself in the office of Mr. Boardman, the dean of men, far too often. He had a paddle he wasn't afraid to use when I got kicked out of class, and, unlike at home, I had no opportunity to stuff newspapers down my trousers.

On one occasion, when the teacher had to briefly step out of the room, I took the opportunity to open the window, scoop up a handful of snow, make a snowball, and hurl it at another student. That was one of about half a dozen times I shuffled down the hall to confront Mr. Boardman.

I started noticing girls when I was still in grade school, but became much more appreciative in junior high. In grade school, I had a crush on Nicky. Janie, my friend and next-door neighbor, was good friends with Nicky. Lovestruck, I plotted with Janie. "Will you walk home with Nicky? When you get to 13th and Elm, I want you to ask her a question."

She agreed and I hid behind a hedge at the designated rendezvous spot. That's when Janie asked her question, "What do you think of Andy?"

I don't remember what Nicky said – I only remember being smitten and hoping she liked me too.

My memories of the three years of junior high are vague. I remember getting interested in cars and engines, especially fast cars. I met Rich Ferdinandson there, who became a great friend I reconnected with years later. I liked shop, a class where I learned about tools and how to make various things. I still have a leather embossed hunting knife sheath that holds my Boy Scout knife. The rest of that time is a blur.

I was a Cub Scout in grade school. My dad wanted me to continue and I almost made it to Life Scout but wasn't motivated to go all the way to Eagle Scout – and I still regret that. Maybe I wasn't just unmotivated, but lazy, or maybe I lacked confidence – probably the latter.

What still stands out for me throughout my school years is testing the limits – and it wasn't necessarily all negative, although those are the occasions that most readily come to mind.

On the positive side, as an adult I've been fired from two volunteer jobs. That doesn't immediately conjure up a positive image, but one Board position I had was with an organization called *Giffords Gun Owners for Safety*. They said my goals didn't align with theirs. Perhaps not, but my aim was to get more gun owners involved, rather than depend almost solely on the impressive person Giffords had picked to head the Colorado group. He spoke well, had excellent credentials, and was doing a good job of lobbying in the Colorado Legislature, but I was pushing Giffords to involve more people and build the organization. I argued that we would have a bigger voice if we could enrol more gun owners and involve them in establishing more gun safety and gun control. We parted ways when they decided I was pushing too hard.

Something similar occurred when I sat on a board for *Next 50*, an organization striving to create a world that values aging. We had 230 million dollars, giving away ten million a year. Problems arose between the staff and the board. Along with another member of the board who was an attorney, I tried to sort through it, but we were both voted out after three years. The reason? We weren't "going with the flow."

But of course, that's me in a nutshell – not going with the flow. When I see something that isn't right, I want to get involved. I don't see a benefit to sitting on the sidelines if I think I can be of some help.

Inherent in me is also the sense of wanting to make my life more interesting and fun. Fooling around, joking, especially telling "dad jokes," being a bit irreverent – these are perhaps more acceptable ways to test limits and create some excitement. But there are times it just feels good to act foolish and to lighten up my life and the lives of those around me. As Maya Angelou said, "My mission in life is not merely to survive, but to thrive; and to do so with some passion, some compassion, some humor, and some style."

For me, testing the limits wasn't just about society's limits – it was my own. I tested and pushed them when I applied to Harvard, first for my master's, and then for my doctorate. I never thought I'd get into Harvard the first time, let alone for a doctorate. That internal testing, which is really courage, led me to starting my own practice twice, and has enabled me to do what I genuinely wanted to do.

Again, from Maya Angelou, "Courage is the most important of the virtues, because without it, no other virtue can be practiced consistently. We can't be kind, true, merciful, generous, or honest."

Whose limits was I testing when I threw or kicked the basketball belonging to the big kids who took over my court? And was I stupid to do that or courageous?

Inside me live two conflicting tendencies. One drives me to be hard on myself and tells me I'm not good enough; the other gives me the confidence to push and never give up, and makes me proud of achieving my goals.

I used to say that I got into the "bad part" of Harvard – the School of Public Health. The "good part" would have been to be accepted as an undergraduate because that's a lot harder. Part of me gets down on myself and accentuates the negatives – like the "bad part" of Harvard. On the other hand, there are times I feel proud of who I am and what I have accomplished. Perhaps most of us go back and forth between these two ends of the continuum.

But I like the more humble side of myself. Maybe my dad saw both sides and was afraid that if he praised me enough it would go to my head. And maybe I like the humble side because that seemed to be what he was aiming for. On the other hand, if he had given me more "atta boys" I might have done better.

Or I might have done worse.

I almost always had a job and when I did, I did it well, even selling door-to-door when I was ten. I was always conscientious, wanting to do a good job. I was also curious – not just about how physical things worked, but also about how business was structured. I approached my jobs from the viewpoint of wanting to learn and a genuine desire to do well. In junior high school, I was a bagger in a supermarket, earning sixty-four cents an hour. I'd pack the brown paper bags carefully, smile at the customers, and occasionally bring the bags out to the customers' cars, sometimes getting a ten or twenty-five cent tip.

I worked in construction one summer during college. The work was physically tougher than anything I'd ever experienced. I operated the pneumatic drill, breaking up the concrete sidewalk, the noise deafening, vibrations coursing through my body. I'd fill a wheelbarrow with mortar and push several hundred pounds up to the bricklayers' site. I remember having one clear thought: *this is backbreaking work.*

Ever since, I've felt considerable empathy for blue collar workers.

One year, I capitalized on my Christmas wreath and ornament work by hiring a couple of younger kids, training them in my sales technique, and sending them out to do the sales. I paid them and took a percentage.

For two years, I sold fireworks with a friend. While they were illegal in Denver, we could sell them in the suburbs around the city. I'd rent a piece of high-traffic vacant land for three weeks leading up to the Fourth of July and buy fireworks from a wholesaler who would also erect a stand with display shelves. I bought a string of lights to make the stand even more visible. In those few weeks, I would make about a thousand dollars. As well as being lucrative, the experience also taught me more about business. The supplier provided value packs of fireworks, but I found I could create my own value packs and make a bigger profit.

In my jobs, my attitude was a complete turn-around from my "prank" persona. I believed in great customer service and a warm approach. These two sides were part of me – and they still are.

I continued to push boundaries after entering East High School in 1958 at age fifteen. The school was an imposing red brick edifice built in the 1920s with an impressive triple arched entrance and a central tower that rivalled government state buildings in its magnificence. If the designers' aim was to instill awe and respect for learning in the student body, they succeeded.

I was scared, intimidated, and overwhelmed. I still didn't know how to study and my confidence continued at a low ebb. I didn't do particularly well, graduating at best with a C-plus average. To get by I tried to copy other students' test answers when I thought I could get away with it, and I still had trouble with math and spelling.

In my first year, my best friend, Robbi, and I were standing on a street corner on the main drag in Denver, when a red '55 or '56 Cadillac convertible cruised by. I yelled, "I just can't stand red Cadillac convertibles."

That was a mistake. The guys were probably ten years older and a lot bigger. We watched them turn the corner, obviously to go around the block and come back for us. Across the street was a Holiday Inn with a diner attached. "Robby," I said. "We've got to duck into that restaurant. Those guys are coming after us."

We walked in and climbed onto stools at the counter. The guys tracked us and came into the diner. One strode over to me. "Were you criticizing my car?"

What could I say to wriggle out of this? Before I could think of something even halfway intelligent, a big guy sitting a few stools down, decided we were two innocents being bullied by a couple of tough guys. He walked over with great purpose. "Leave these kids alone!" he said.

Saved!

One time in English class, we had an assignment to read a book and write a report. I wasn't into reading books and even less into writing about them. But I picked up and read a book about World War II. It grabbed my attention so thoroughly that I didn't mind writing the report. My teacher, Mr. Koerber, commented on my paper, "See what you can do, Andy, when you set your mind to it? This was a really good report. You should read more books like this!'

That memory stands out because I so rarely received compliments on academic achievements. I was proud and gratified, and I wish I could say it was some sort of turning point. It wasn't, but I know his words had their positive effects much later.

One day, during my second semester of high school, I was at home, not doing anything in particular, when I looked through the front window and saw a group of guys pull up in cars, jump out and hustle up the walk to the front door. I didn't recognize any of them, didn't know who they were, or why they were there.

Oh god! I must have done something! They're coming after me!

I ran out of the room, down the hall and out the back door. I didn't know what they were going to do to me. I only knew I had to get away.

I was utterly wrong. The boys represented a Jewish high school fraternity and were there to give me a bid to join. I was stunned. I'd never heard of the group and knew nothing about it. But they wanted me! I wondered why they'd chosen me but never asked.

Although it didn't sit well with me to be part of an exclusive group, I took them up on their offer because it made me feel good. and I'm still friends with some of the guys I met there. Taking the pledge meant a period of initiation that included paddling and basically doing whatever the senior boys told me to.

The fraternity, Phi Tau Pi, was the Denver branch of a national fraternity. One requirement of the pledge was to learn the Greek alphabet and to be able to repeat it within three seconds, or after lighting a match before the flame burnt a finger. I worked on it, mastered it, and could still repeat it quickly until just a few years ago.

In my senior year, I attended a party at a friend's house the night before New Year's Eve. We all generally drank beer and hard liquor, and on this particular night I drank vodka directly from the bottle. I have a vague memory of standing at the front door of my house, my friends holding me up. They told me later that they also held me up under the shower, hoping a rush of water would sober me up. It didn't, so they dropped me in my bed. My mom, worried that I'd throw up and aspirate, sat in my room most of the night.

The next day, my parents let me know they weren't happy with me. And there I was, feeling perfectly fine.

My friend, Robbi, was also a member of the fraternity, and our relationship flourished as we grew closer. Many years later, in my early seventies, I read on Facebook that Robbi had died in a car accident while driving home after providing oral surgery services to people in a rural area in Texas. I flew to Dallas for his funeral. Seeing his casket made losing him all too real. I miss him to this day.

I liked some of the frat members but there were others I didn't care for at all. Certain things about them made me feel uncomfortable about being associated with them, especially because we were all Jewish.

As I noted earlier in this story, the Jewish identity question has always been a challenge for me. Ellen, who also comes from a reformed Jewish background, has typically been prouder of her religion and culture and has celebrated the major holidays more consistently.

However, over the years, I've become prouder of my faith. On occasion, I even get emotional about some of the ideas that are highlighted in a service or holiday. A trip to Israel to visit our daughter had a deep influence on my attitude. It was the first time I felt that sense of pride as I got to know the people and saw and appreciated all they had done there. The experience of being surrounded by other Jews and not having any trepidation about the possibility of antisemitism was a significant first for me. I doubt I'm alone in that experience.

The Jewish fraternity quickly became the core of my high school social life.

With my dad's encouragement – and possibly urging – I went out for the football team. I knew the coach from Little League, and I'll never forget his words to me after he'd cut a number of people from the team: "Andy, you're not trying. You can play with these guys – you have since you were a kid, but if you don't ramp it up, I'm going to cut you too."

One last cut to the team came up, and the person he cut was me. I've reflected on that incident. I believe we do that as we get older, often gaining greater insight into our actions of the past. My first reaction back then was to blame my dad for pushing me to try out. I was rebelling against him. Yes, perhaps I was, but that was only part of it. As hard as it is for me to say this or write it, I think I was afraid to compete at that level. For a long time, it was simply easier for me not to acknowledge that and just blame my dad.

When the coach cut me, I think there was a genuine sense of relief, but underneath that was something else – a realization of sorts: *what have I done?*

That gut-wrenching feeling plummeted deep into my stomach later that year when our team was playing for the state championship, and all the guys I'd played with in Little League were out on the field with the glory, the girls, the cheerleaders, and the deserved accolades while I was sitting in the stands.

What did I do? I should be out there with my friends!

When I look back at my life, that occasion stands out as one of my regrets. Regret haunts me – I have so many. As a hospice volunteer, starting in 2000, I worked with at least twenty or thirty people nearing the end of their lives. During our conversations, I asked almost all of them if they had any regrets and what those might be. Most said they had none.

I've thought about that. Why do I have so many? I have no answer. Looking back on my life as I write this memoir, I find myself re-thinking and re-appraising my actions, motivations, thoughts, and emotions. I have always been analytical and transparent; my emotions and thoughts have rarely been hidden, a trait that can be an asset or a liability.

I've been introspective, but only in the last couple of decades or so have I focused on applying my insights and really committing myself to doing better in relating to my family. In describing me, Ellen has said she thinks I've become more introspective as I've gotten older. I've certainly recognized errors I've made, and have worked hard to become a better person.

Perhaps that's why, when I examine my life, I see where I came up short of my own expectations. I'm a pretty confident person, but there are things I wish I could do over again. I'm amazed that so many people don't think like that about their past. Don't they think their lives could have been better?

In high school, I continued to pull pranks, some of which did not contribute to making my life better. I lost a girlfriend partly because of my antics. She was a lovely popular person who even became head girl at the school. Honestly, I thought I was dating above my pay grade. However, going through my old year books, the comments I read mention that I was a nice guy, that I was fun, sweet, caring, and compassionate. Most people didn't see the wild part of me. Clearly, I was the person most aware of my failings. I probably came across as being a bit shy, so they probably thought the best of me, unaware of some of the huge stunts I pulled, like the time I dropped into an Oldsmobile dealership to pick up a part for my car when I spotted a big ring of keys behind the counter and stole it. It turned out that some of the keys on the ring were masters to General Motors products, enabling me to unlock and drive almost any GM vehicle.

I used them to visit the *Midnight Auto Supply,* a term used for going out at night and stealing from people's cars. When my radio didn't work because of a burned-out tube, I went out, found a car similar to mine, and took the tube off the radio. I took floor mats, and one time, when my friends and I attended Frontier Days in Cheyenne, Wyoming and couldn't find a parking place, I drove a car out of its spot, and parked my vehicle in its place.

My school day ended one period earlier than others, which gave me about thirty minutes to use my master key to unlock the gorgeous, fast, white Corvette convertible my girlfriend drove to school, and take it for a ride. I'd done that a couple of times when she asked me one night, "Andy, do you know anything about my car? Were you driving it?"

I admitted I had – and she ended our relationship. I felt an ache I hadn't experienced before. I was sitting in the kitchen with my mom – hurt, depressed, and mopey, when she said that first loves hold a place in our hearts forever. She told me she'd been engaged to another man when she met my dad. She broke up with him to marry my father who she'd fallen in love with, but she said she'd never quite erased her guilt – and Bill still occupied a special place in her heart.

Interestingly, Ellen and I met under similar circumstances. She was dating a man who was on a motorcycle tour of Europe during the summer we met. When she stopped receiving letters from him, she assumed he'd dropped her – perhaps met another woman in France or Germany. Ellen and I fell in love. When her boyfriend came back from Europe, eager to re-unite with Ellen, he explained that there'd been a postal strike on the continent. Like my mother, Ellen still lives with a sense of guilt over breaking his heart.

Living close to my maternal grandparents was a gift with lifelong benefits. Although I was fifteen when my grandfather, Boppa, died, and twenty when my grandmother, YiYi died, I was able to spend special time with them.

During high school I often took my grandmother grocery shopping in my '36 Ford. She was an extroverted soul – everybody was her friend, and while I enjoyed being with her, I was also a bit embarrassed when she would strike up conversations with so many people and introduce me to her "store friends," like the butcher and the cashier.

YiYi had a captivating laugh that drew people to her. She often told me about the importance of being loving and caring towards other people. I suspect she was aware that some of my behavior did not always demonstrate love, and hoped I would take her words to heart. I also think she genuinely believed in the idea that "love begets love," a lesson my mother repeated.

I remember family dinners on Sunday nights at either my grandparents' or parents' home with some of their close friends. We sat around a big dining room table with my grandfather at one end and my grandmother at the other.

My grandparents' cook made a pie for President Eisenhower and his wife Mamie, who grew up a few blocks from their house. We were always excited when the president and his wife came to Denver, and we would drive by her home to gawk at the secret service men guarding it.

Having my family around me, listening to them, and being part of the fun and conversations meant a lot to me. I have a memory of eating dinner with my parents and my girlfriend's mother, who I wanted to impress. But my parents decided to prank me. My dad, who was an expert with the carving knife, sliced a piece of ham, picked it up, and threw it across the table to my girlfriend's mother. I was mortified! They laughed. I suppose I had it coming, given all the stunts I'd pulled over the years!

CHAPTER 6

TURNING POINTS

In high school we had a game we played called *One Up Three Down* that went like this: Chucky, a small tough guy, would go into a drive-through restaurant, yell obscenities at high school kids in other cars – enough to make them chase him – and he'd peel out, tearing down a side street. Meanwhile, three of us would be hiding in the car and jump up when the other car pulled over. For some reason, we thought that was great fun – a big adrenaline rush.

Taking risks was part of the game. Not far from my house was a job site where big earth-moving equipment was left overnight. One time, near midnight, I hot-wired one of them – easy to do back then because the ignition wasn't covered and you could start the engine using a piece of tin foil to connect the wires. The engine jolted into action, startlingly loud in the still of the night. I managed to get it into gear and drive it a couple of feet before porch lights flicked on up and down the street, doors opened, and the neighbors came out to investigate.

I ran like hell.

Denver had a popular bowling alley and indoor swimming pool complex called Celebrity Sports Center. We spent a good deal of time there, especially playing on the pinball machines. It was also the site where my friends and I pulled another prank. The entry and exit doors could be locked, and we spent many weekend evenings locking either the entry or exit doors. The various reactions of people who stepped on the platform expecting the door to open automatically were our entertainment.

East High School became badly overcrowded during my two-year tenure. In response, Denver built more schools, one of which, George Washington High School, opened in time for my senior year. Many of my friends stayed in my old school, others, including my fraternity, came with me to George Washington. I managed to graduate with a C or C-plus average, but I had no strong sense of what to do next. College seemed the obvious step, but I didn't think my grades would get me into the University of Colorado, so I applied to and was accepted by Colorado State University in Fort Collins.

Because I had to declare a major, I chose business without really knowing why. And I continued to test the limits. One time, I ignited the bottom of a pizza box with lighter fluid and slid it under the door of a room down the hall. Another time, the guys in the room next door went away for the weekend and locked their door. We were on the second floor. I scrambled out our window and managed to climb in through their window. After messing up their room, I climbed back into ours. The guys came back, unlocked their door and stood back in shock. How was it possible that someone had entered their room? The door was locked!

One incident was humiliating. During the fraternity rush, my dorm roommate, a handsome, confident guy named Reno, visited one with me. I was feeling intimidated and insecure. Not Reno – he was in the reception line in front of me and put his hand out with great self-assurance. "Hi! I'm Reno M. Nice to meet you"

I was up next, and I was so out of my body that I put my hand out and said, "Hi! I'm Reno M. Nice to meet you."

I did not get a bid for that fraternity. But the truth is, I didn't really want one anyway. I'd done that and had enough of it in high school.

I liked a couple of my classes, and I believe they may have been responsible for starting me on a path to actually getting interested in learning. One was a class on current events, and I probably have my mom to thank for that. She attended a current events group of women that would meet and discuss the news of the day. I suspect some of that interest and curiosity rubbed off on me.

I was required to take ROTC, and took part in the air force program. I liked quite a bit about that: we had uniforms and even though it was the Air Force and not the Marine Corps, it had a strong appeal. We learned about airplanes and aerodynamics, which played to my interest in motors and how things worked generally. My grades were probably Bs and Cs.

My Denver girlfriend, who I met just before starting college, was likely one of the reasons I didn't study as hard as I should have. She was my real first love, and I spent a lot of weekends travelling from Fort Collins to Denver to see her.

She was two years younger, an excellent student, popular, cute, and exhibited a lot of depth. In some ways, I'm sure she influenced me to take my studies more seriously.

After my first year at Colorado State, I transferred to the University of Colorado in Boulder so I could be closer to her. But CU was tough and I found myself on academic probation the first year.

My girlfriend was the impetus for a lot of decisions I made for the next three years. My parents liked her and her family but they didn't want to see me wrapping my life around her. They thought I was missing out on the college experience, so they pulled some strings to get me accepted into Tulane University in Louisiana. They gave me the news while we were driving somewhere, me in the back seat, unable to hold back my tears. They argued it would be good for me to get away and be on my own.

I refused to go. They then asked me to agree to see my girlfriend only once a month or so, even asking me to sign a paper stating the agreement. "We want you to be on campus and enjoy campus life," they said.

I signed, but the agreement meant nothing to me. I continued to see her as much as possible. In retrospect, I understand their viewpoint. At the time, it was untenable.

My first year at CU, I lived in a motel with a friend I knew from grade school. He left at the end of the first semester, and I moved in with a friend from my high school fraternity. We had a nice cabin abutting a stream in the mountains just west of Boulder. The living situation was great until I had a run-in with another guy who was also renting a room. He routinely left his dirty dishes in the communal kitchen sink, and one evening I asked him to clean them up. Instantly, he pulled a knife out of the sink and threw it at me. I left after that and moved in with another group of friends from high school.

The following year, I lived in an apartment with my old friend and partner in crime, Robbi.

Figure 5 Robbi and me 1961

He played the guitar, and I spent many nights over many years in various venues getting lost listening to him sing folk songs about relationships and the human condition. They never ceased to engross me. That year, I found many of my classes interesting and began to take my studies more seriously. But we still found time for fun, and more pranks, the most notable one occurring toward the end of finals week shortly before the Christmas break.

Robbi and I drove about eight hundred and seventy miles straight through from Boulder to St Louis in my 1955 Chevy, three-speed on the column, with overdrive, and a souped-up 265 cu engine. Our plan was to surprise my parents who were already there visiting my grandmother and not expecting me. Before we left, we put my ski racks on the car in order to look cool. We got to St. Louis mid-morning and drove to the apartment where my grandmother lived. As we pulled up, we spotted my parents walking down the street toward the apartment building.

I put on Robbi's big peacoat, turned the enormous collar up around my neck, lit a cigar, and swaggered toward them. I passed by them, turned around, and said, "Hi."

My mother turned to my dad and said, "If I wasn't sure Andy was in Boulder studying for finals, I could swear he just walked by us."

When I moved to Boulder, I bought a motorcycle, sold it, and bought another one. When my parents came to visit and take me out to dinner, I moved the motorcycle to the back of the apartment house where I lived, knowing they would disapprove. But my father was too sharp. "Andy," he said. "What's the oil stain on the concrete outside your door?"

"I have a motorcycle."

They weren't happy. Looking back, I can see all the anxiety I caused them, and I'm sorry about it, but I continued being a prankster. One night during finals week, Robbi and I siphoned gas from a car into a waste basket. Siphoning gas was one of the more dubious skills I'd acquired and practiced quite a lot during high school. On this occasion, I wanted to see what would happen if we poured it into the pool of our apartment building. We tipped it in and struck a match.

Whoosh!

The flames shot up two stories. Fire trucks with sirens blaring arrived to douse the flames. The next morning, the building managers were scrubbing the blackened tiles on the side of the pool. Robbi and I volunteered to help. They thought we were awfully nice to lend a hand, never knowing we were the cause of the damage.

I think I was always aware when I'd done something wrong, even when I was quite young. Later in life, when I was stressed out at work and got impatient with my daughters Sara and Becky, or Ellen, my wife, I was cognizant that I was out of control, but I just didn't know what to do to stop it. Maybe that's the source of my regrets.

Gradually, my education became more important to me, thanks in part to my mother, her current events group, Great Decisions, and an influential conference. Every year since 1948, the University of Colorado has hosted the Conference on World Affairs, featuring panel discussions among experts in international affairs and other areas. It was founded by Howard Higman, a brilliant sociologist, and featured some of the top thinkers in the world like Buckminster Fuller and Dag Hammarskjold. My mother would drive up from Denver and we would attend some of the seminars. Listening to the panel discussions inspired me and opened my mind to the joy of knowledge. The conference was a piece of an intricate puzzle that started coming together for me in those years and that would eventually turn me around.

Another major turning point was a class Higman taught called Group Structure and Behavior. He had a reputation for drinking, and I still have the image in my mind of him entering the classroom and weaving his way down the aisle to the front of the room. But he was a wonderful lecturer, talking about group dynamics, and how culture and context affect behavior, attitudes, and values. That class played a major role in making me a better student. I went from academic probation to being on the dean's list in my junior and senior years.

I also took History of Colorado classes, probably inspired by my own family history, and I thoroughly enjoyed my classes on political science as well as abnormal psychology, where I became fascinated by hypnosis. One time, I tried putting my roommate in a trance. To this day, I don't know if I succeeded or if he was pulling my leg.

Before my senior year, I entered a summer program *The Sociology of Mental Health,* that had a major impact on my choice of profession – and the rest of my life. I also became close to Al, who was in the same program, and who has been a close friend since. The program took place at the Fort Logan Mental Health Center, considered one of the best psychiatric facilities in the world at that time. People came from all around the country and the world to study its innovative methods of working with patients.

The center followed a concept of therapeutic community, meaning it provided group therapy almost exclusively. People were encouraged to interact appropriately and effectively and were rewarded for it. The patients had their own government with meetings each morning that involved all twenty or thirty people in the unit, talking about how they were feeling and how they were getting along. Everything they did revolved around the concept of community.

My experience there was life-changing. Each week, the staff had a "feelings" meeting, based on the idea that how the staff got along and felt about their work and the patients influenced the success of the entire community. I didn't know it at the time, but this concept, called the Stanton Schwartz Effect, had been identified in the 1950s, named after psychiatrist Alfred H. Stanton and sociologist Morris S. Schwartz. Schwartz was the subject of Mitch Albom's best-seller, *Tuesdays with Morrie.*

I worked with Morrie at Harvard where he supervised a group I was part of that was helping de-institutionalize a large state mental health hospital and transform it into a mental health center. In the 1950s, Schwartz had written a book titled *The Mental Hospital,* a pioneering study that examined a hospital as a social organization. But his main concept was the Stanton Schwartz Effect, and this was what we were doing our best to implement at Fort Logan – deal with the issues and interpersonal relationship challenges of the staff as well as the patients, knowing one would affect the other.

The summer course also required a certain amount of research. The other student and I focused on the feelings meetings, trying to determine whether the meetings had an effect on staff conflicts. It was my first experience with research and I found it fascinating and rewarding.

Our unit team included a psychiatrist, who was our formal leader, a psychologist, a social worker, and a head nurse. The psychiatrist was a fairly passive person. Harold Parker, the social worker, effectively ran the unit. He became my mentor, playing a decisive role in my choice to get a master's in social work. He was good with patients, helpful to all of us, and key to making me feel good about choosing social work as a career, despite the fact it had a reputation for being a woman's profession.

My dad wasn't especially happy about my choice, mostly because it didn't pay well, but I was determined, largely because of my admiration for Harold. One of the patients I worked with was a girl my age who had jumped off a viaduct crossing a highway through Denver. She landed on top of a car and survived the suicide attempt. I wanted to help and to understand her motivation for wanting to end her life. I probably cared too much. I couldn't get her off my mind. I can't remember what happened – but something involving her, and Harold asked her in the most straightforward way, "Why did you do what you did? What's going on?"

And just like that, my notions on therapy got turned around. Weren't you supposed to be subtle and round-about in your questioning? Harold just got to the point – no pussy-footing for him.

To this day, when I'm working with someone and I find I'm not being as direct as I could be, I remember Harold's words.

My last year of college, I lived at home and got a job at the airport on the ramp, meaning I loaded and unloaded baggage. The job paid the money I needed and provided free airline passes. I wanted to fly to New York where my girlfriend now lived, but our relationship began to deteriorate, and I didn't go. My mother was the only one who used my pass, flying round trip to Chicago.

In 1965, during the summer after my college graduation, I got a position as a recreational therapist at the National Jewish Hospital, a health institution for kids with asthma. It was a great job for me because I'd always loved kids and I had practice as a day camp counselor.

The entire experience was wonderful, but I particularly remember an adorable little Alaskan boy, about four or five, with a bad case of asthma. When his birthday came, he waited in great anticipation for his parents to call. He waited and waited. Finally, it was time for bed. I was working late when the phone rang. I woke him up, happy to give him good news.

"Your parents are on the phone."

He absorbed the information, gasped, and immediately collapsed in a major attack, his face turning blue. I don't remember how he recovered, but what stuck with me was the incredible power of psychology. He'd had so much hope all day, and then the disappointment of not receiving a birthday call – and then, when they did, his entire body reacted seriously and dramatically.

I befriended another counselor that summer – Floyd Westerman, who is also known as Floyd Red Crow Westerman, a Dakota Sioux who had been in the Marine Corps and was famous later in life as a folk singer, political activist, and actor, notably playing one of the leading chief rolls in *Dances with Wolves*, the Oscar-winning Kevin Costner film. He came to my house once, playing his guitar and singing, holding us all spellbound. I tried to track him down once and found he'd died of leukemia. I still feel sad that we didn't stay in contact. He was a special man. I remember with particular fondness the CD he cut singing Johnny Cash songs.

CHAPTER 7

GRADUATE SCHOOL

In 1965, I graduated from the University of Colorado, but didn't attend my commencement. The school was big and impersonal and the official ceremony meant little to me.

I applied to graduate school to study social work, partly because I'd been inspired not only by Harold Parker, but also Dorothea Spellman, a professor of social work at the University of Denver who served for years with my dad on the Auraria Community Center Board. She was one of the founders of the American Civil Liberties Union (ACLU), and when I applied to graduate schools in social work, she wrote recommendations. She never failed to encourage me in my curiosity and desire to learn. I still have cards she sent me, one containing a quote from the Supreme Court Justice, Oliver Wendell Holmes Jr., "Success is not the position where you are standing, but which direction you are going."

I was equally inspired by my parents' volunteer work and the dinner-table discussions about Planned Parenthood, civil rights, and poverty. I was also pleased it was only a two-year program. I wanted to be a therapist and this seemed the shortest route to that goal. I applied to several schools, was accepted by most, and enrolled in New York University (NYU) in New York City, mostly because my girlfriend was attending nearby Sarah Lawrence College and I was still trying to make the relationship work.

The next two years were packed with experiences I couldn't have imagined. First, I had to find a place to live. A friend from Denver let me crash on the floor of his apartment while I searched for more permanent housing.

I was utterly overwhelmed – a young man coming from Denver where people smiled and waved hello on the streets entering a maelstrom where people brushed by you in a determined frenzy to get to their next appointment, and eye contact was considered an invasion of privacy. I was frightened – and sad because my grandmother, who I'd loved dearly, had recently died. I struggled in vain to find a place to live. And then, my friend's mother died and he returned to Denver, leaving me with the apartment – a fifth-floor walk-up in Greenwich Village, the hub of the hippie movement.

I was still a Denver boy, feeling alone and scared, but smiling and saying hi to strangers when they seemed friendly. But I had questions. Why was I still feeling sad about my grandmother and intimidated by the city? I started seeing a psychotherapist to get answers, finding the sessions healing and helpful.

I was grateful for my small apartment, heated by radiators that would clang and bang late at night. I called the superintendent, who did nothing to stop the noise that woke me constantly. When I obtained the owner's phone number, I called – still nothing. My only solution to my sleepless nights was to wake him up whenever I was roused from sleep by the infernal noise. I called him at 3 a.m. "Your radiators are waking me up."

He fixed them.

That year, 1965, was when I tried drugs for the first time, specifically, marijuana. I shared a joint with a woman I'd met at Fort Logan. "I'm not feeling anything," I said, thinking this whole "getting high" thing was a total bust.

Still insisting I felt nothing, I walked with my friend into a bakery to buy some donuts. Standing in front of the cashier, I watched him place the donuts into a box and close the lid. Slowly, his hand wound the string around the width of the box, then, even more slowly, he wrapped it around the length. He handed me the box and instantly, I felt an overwhelming urge to run. I dashed out the store and down the street, feeling the air caressing my face, the wind rushing through my hair. What a glorious sensation! At some point I stopped, elated. My friend caught up with me. "Andy," she panted. "Stop running! What are you doing?"

Oh. Maybe I was feeling something after all.

To digress briefly, my mother said the same thing many years later when I shared some pot with her. "I don't feel anything," she insisted, although, oddly, she couldn't stop eating.

NYU gave me a great education. I loved my classes and my teachers. I read everything on the syllabus and beyond including most of Freud and other seminal thinkers in the field of human development, systems theory, and psychotherapy. I was a sponge, absorbing everything I could. It was all interesting – social work, therapy, and all the factors that influence us, like childhood experiences and the systems we come in contact with. I was reading, not only to learn more about others, but to understand myself and what motivated me. I didn't have any earth-shattering insights, but many smaller ones, particularly as to how various systems impact us, whether it's society, the family, organizations, education, or government. Studying those dynamics and therapy helped me better understand my family and its influence.

The mid-sixties weren't just about hippies, civil rights, Vietnam, and summers of love – those were also the years when students wanted more representation in their schools. I was elected class vice president and I recall talking to the dean - but about what? Possibly making our studies more relevant to the times?

My classes in both years included field work. Two or three days a week I was out working with the public. The first year, I was a probation officer in the southeast Bronx. If I'd been intimidated in Greenwich Village, I was certainly not prepared for the southeast Bronx, which was low income, overwhelmingly African-American, and a generally tough neighborhood. But scared as I was, I had great experiences with my clients.

I'll never forget my first, a Puerto Rican man who had been lured to New York City by the Catholic Church with promises of a job and a better life for himself and his family. The point for the church was to bring more Catholics to their area, but the promise of work was an empty one. After a fruitless search, he went on welfare. He then found a job he genuinely liked, not knowing the rules forbade him from working while he was on welfare. He was put on probation – this well-intentioned man who was trying to make a good life for his family.

At the close of my first year at NYU, I learned about the Lisle Fellowship, founded in 1936 in upstate New York by a pair of Methodist ministers. The fellowship had a long history in the field of global intercultural experiences. I'd been wanting to go to Europe for the summer and this seemed a perfect opportunity to make it more meaningful, rather than just traveling as a tourist. I was accepted to study in Denmark for the month of July. I convinced a friend and classmate to come with me, so I bought a Volkswagen I planned to pick up in Brussels and drive around the continent during the month of June.

I flew to London first, wearing a pretty spiffy seersucker suit. From there, I hopped a plane to Brussels to meet my friend and pick up the vehicle. After purchasing the car, I stopped at the dealership's men's room. To my considerable consternation, I couldn't zip up my fly. I tried and tried but no – it was broken. I'd smoothly handled traveling in Europe for the first time, not speaking the language, and not having any sleep for twenty-four hours, but the broken zipper was just too much.

What to do? I found a safety pin somewhere in my bag, did my best with it, and shuffled out of the washroom, holding my hand in front of me just to be sure.

The purpose of our stay in Denmark was to learn about the culture and world issues. We met students from South Africa, Denmark, Sweden, Germany, and the United States. We were given three experiences, called "deputations." My first was spending several nights with a family of farmers, who I am still friends with on Facebook.

I remember getting up at 4 a.m. to help the farmer load the tractor with cabbages before taking them to the exchange. He spoke no English, but his daughter served as an able translator. He told me he was in the Danish resistance during World War II and showed me his old rifle. He also told me a few stories from that time, but sadly, I've lost the details.

My second deputation involved learning about Denmark's relationship with Greenland. I was able to talk to Greenland's ambassador to Denmark and several other officials as well as politicians who also talked to us about current events.

For our third deputation, we visited an institution that housed handicapped children. I was horrified – struck to the heart by seeing children who couldn't walk or talk. I'd never been exposed to that kind of suffering, and though I knew it was a valuable experience, it was also hard to take in.

Sue, an American girl in the program, had a family friend in the German Parliament. During a conversation, I must have mentioned that I was Jewish and interested in my family's background. At some point, my dad had mentioned that some family members had been killed by the Nazis. Sue obtained a letter of introduction from the government official that I took to a couple of German police stations.

I recall sitting at a table in the basement of one station sifting through records. I gleaned a bit of information, enough to tell me that one of my relatives had been killed, probably in Auschwitz, and that whole murderous Nazi era suddenly became real and personal.

In August, at the end of the fellowship, I spent another four weeks driving around Europe. I very much wanted to go to Berlin. On the way, I picked up an Israeli hitchhiker, also on his way there. We stopped at the border to East Germany and showed our passports to the armed guards while staring up at the guard towers manned by men in uniforms with automatic weapons.

Suddenly, Amir, the hitchhiker, burst into a rant about the evil Germans. I could feel the instant grip of fear in my throat and belly.

"Either stop or get out of the car," I said. "I don't want to get shot or jailed."

Thankfully, he stopped.

In Berlin, my most vivid memory is passing through Checkpoint Charlie, the famous border crossing symbolizing the separation of east and west. The contrast was shocking. While West Berlin was an alive, cosmopolitan, sophisticated city, the East Berlin streets were almost empty, buildings still riddled with bullet and shrapnel holes, and people hurrying grimly to their offices or homes.

It's impossible to overestimate the effects of foreign travel on deepening our understanding of ourselves, people, and the world. It's good to be reminded that not everyone thinks as we do or lives life as we do. Intellectually, that may be obvious, but to experience it firsthand, is personally expanding.

CHAPTER 8

DANGER

I brought my VW back from Brussels before settling in for my second year at NYU. Having a car in the city gave me the freedom I needed – the possibility of escape from the concrete sidewalks, steel towers, and harried crowds to the nature and solitude I often craved. But while New York still overwhelmed me at times, there was also something about it that drew me in – the city never slept. I could step out my door at any time to see people walking on the streets, hear jazz floating out of a cellar piano bar and drifting across a sidewalk like autumn leaves, or smell the meaty grease of sizzling hot dogs from a nearby food truck.

I had no trouble finding places to park my little blue bug. I had Colorado plates and there were no computers in those days to link plates to parking tickets. When I ran up four hundred dollars in fines, I didn't give it a thought.

In my second year of studies, my field work involved working at Hillside, a private psychiatric hospital. I didn't have the same connection with or admiration for my second-year supervisor as I'd had in my first year. She was married to a psychiatrist who worked at Hillside, and her attitude was clearly opposed to mine. She believed social workers were subservient to psychiatrists. I disagreed. I thought both roles were equally important and each deserved respect. However, I still enjoyed my classes and delving into the subjects I was studying.

In 1967, I received my Master of Social Work (MSW). At the time there were three concentrations, or fields of practice. Mine was casework, although some called it psychiatric social work.

In 1967, Vietnam was very much in the news. I didn't agree with our involvement in what I considered a civil war, and made the decision not to go. I have questioned that choice to this day. I grew up with a father I looked up to – a hero who volunteered for the Marine Corps. From the time I was a little boy, I wanted to wear that uniform and grow up to be a pilot. I wanted to be as brave and honorable as my dad. But I couldn't reconcile that image with the politics of Vietnam. Why were we even there?

I wasn't about to go to Canada, so I had to find another option. I searched for alternative avenues and while scanning through documents at the NYU library, I found one with the Commissioned Corps, the uniformed service branch of the United States Public Health Service (USPHSCC).

The USPHSCC is one of the eight uniformed services of the United States that is not an armed service. Its primary mission is the protection, promotion, and advancement of health and safety of the general public. It had its beginnings with the creation of the Marine Hospital Fund in 1798, which later was reorganized in 1871 as the Marine Hospital Service.

I applied and was accepted as a Lieutenant Junior Grade, the most junior commissioned officer rank, assigned to Saint Elizabeths Hospital in Washington D.C., a psychiatric hospital housing about six thousand people.

I deliberately call the residents people and not patients. I have always objected to the term patient, particularly in mental health situations. Certainly, there are many sociological explanations for the role of the patient and caregiver, but in my mind, the word patient is too loaded with demeaning associations. If you're a patient, there must be something wrong with you, and you're needy, and perhaps not as capable as those providing care. I have always referred to those I am working with as clients or, preferably, persons.

The late sixties marked the heyday of mental health treatment in the United States and probably around the world. The emphasis had shifted to de-institutionalization – recognizing that warehousing people in huge hospitals wasn't in the best interests of the people living there. These institutions operated like autonomous cities with their own laundries, grounds, kitchens, and even governance.

My assignment was to the foster care division that was responsible for finding houses for those discharged from the hospital. The position held little interest for me. I wanted to be on the front lines and requested a transfer. With some effort on my part and a certain amount of luck, I was re-assigned to the William Alanson White Unit, a new and innovative in-patient unit serving Anacostia, a low-income historical district in southeast Washington D.C. with a majority African-American population.

It was considered the hospital's elite wing, an in-patient locked unit with a special relationship with the National Institute of Mental Health, part of the National Institutes of Health. It was the avant-garde arm of the federal government trying to improve health and mental health care.

I was fresh out of school. The psychiatrist heading the unit, just out of his residency at Yale, was only a few years older and we quickly developed a special professional and personal relationship. He gave me a lot of freedom and encouragement to do what I wanted, always showing great confidence in me. Based on my experience at Fort Logan, I started a patient government while also doing a lot of individual and couples therapy. Part of my focus was researching psycho-therapeutic approaches to people who were psychotic and those diagnosed with schizophrenia.

I was in my element, doing something similar to what I had done during my summer at Fort Logan that had made such a deep impression on me. The attitude of the staff in the unit meshed closely with my own thoughts and feelings.

Some experiences in my two years there are etched in my memory. One can still bring tears.

One man in our unit had never felt loved or appreciated. He was a big bear of a man, with all the softness and gentleness associated with a panda or teddy. But he was alone in the world – no relatives or family – and well-liked by everyone he came in contact with. He'd been psychotic, but medication had made an enormous difference, and we believed he was ready to leave the hospital.

I got involved in starting a halfway house where he would live. In fact, he was its first resident. It was the right thing to do, but the resident psychiatrist and I made one major mistake: we'd made no provision for the possibility that the house mother might be unable to fulfill her duties.

Our patient left for the halfway house reluctantly. Our unit had become his home, one of the first places he'd ever felt accepted and wanted. Then, the woman who owned the house, became ill and he had to come back to the hospital. He settled back in, but then we sent him to the halfway house once again. He never arrived.

They found his body in the Anacostia River. He'd jumped off the bridge.

We tried to understand what had happened. What could we have done differently? How could we have handled it better? The only answer we had was that pushing him out triggered his feelings of being unloved and rejected. It had been hard for him to leave us the first time. The second time had been too much.

I wanted to help expand our unit's ability to help and be involved in the community we served, so I contacted a recreational center serving youth with the intention of consulting with them. As part of my effort, I reached out to Archie Ward, a sociologist who worked at St Elizabeths hospital. I remember looking at a big wall map of census tracks in Anacostia on the wall of his office that listed interesting data in each track. I believe I expressed my interest in continuing my education so I could have more impact and advance my career.

That conversation and several that followed turned out to be pivotal in my life. He told me about Alexander Leighton, a psychiatrist, sociologist, and anthropologist, who headed a department at Harvard that focused on the connections between communities and psychological disorders. I'd never thought of myself as qualified or capable of attending a place like Harvard, but a few months later, I applied to several doctoral programs. Harvard was one of them.

I met another memorable person at the hospital – a woman about my age who was psychotic and constantly hallucinating. She was married to a well-known folk singer, and I was into folk music, so perhaps that was part of the attraction. Her father-in-law, a Native American, was also quite famous, both as a folk-singer and author. I attempted psychotherapy sessions with her despite the opinion most held that you can't do therapy with people who are psychotic. I read everything I could about how to conduct this sort of therapy, but honestly, I don't think I gave her a lot of help. Regardless, I wanted to make a difference in her life, and the experience was intense.

Our focus at the hospital was to discharge people as soon as possible. The average stay was seven days, which was revolutionary at the time. We wanted to resolve their issues so they could move back into the world with some kind of aftercare provided. So many people we saw had issues and struggles with other people. My focus on the interpersonal and systemic aspects of psychiatric and psychological disorders that I had studied at NYU was reinforced. Many times, men would come to us feeling deeply depressed with issues that could easily be related to problems in their marriage. We would bring in their spouse, get them communicating, and put their relationship back on track so the men could get out and on with their lives.

I've published quite a few papers in my career, but I think I'm most proud of my first one, published in 1972. I used my studies from my first year at Harvard as the theoretical background for what we did in our in-patient unit. The paper I wrote was for a Harvard course called, *The Sociology of Organizations.*

The psychiatrist whose office was next to mine and who was debuting a new journal titled *Psychiatric Annals*, entered my office one day after reading my paper. He told me it was very good and could he pay me seventy-five dollars to publish it in his journal?

I was pretty excited about that. My first published paper – and I was even being paid for it!

I liked living in Washington D.C. The weather wasn't great – hot and humid in the summers and cold in the winters, but I met interesting people, some who worked on the hill for various senators and congress people and some who had ordinary jobs like I did. I had good friends of both stripes, one who I am still in contact with today.

I bought another motorcycle that I loved riding on the weekends. I also enjoyed going out at night. I lived in southeast Washington, a largely African-American neighbourhood, near a small bar that featured entertainment at night. For a long time, the small stage belonged to Roberta Flack. On at least twenty occasions, I paid the $2.50 cover charge for myself and my date, just to sit in the dark smoky interior to hear Roberta Flack's voice reverberating off the ceiling and walls, mesmerizing us. Her songs, her voice, and her lyrics utterly captivated me. *The First Time Ever I Saw Your Face,* was the song Ellen and I chose for the first dance at our wedding. It still has the power to give me goosebumps.

April 4, 1968. The date is etched forever on my mind. – the day Martin Luther King Jr. was assassinated. I remember standing on a hill in the grounds surrounding the Saint Elizabeths hospital with the psychiatrist I worked with and a clergyman who worked on the ward. From our vantage point, we could see smoke rising up over northwest Washington where the riots were taking place. "You probably shouldn't go home," they said, knowing I lived near the area.

"I'm okay," I said. "I'm going home."

I got into my VW and drove through Anacostia and pulled up to a stoplight, braking a short distance behind the car in front.

"There's a honky!"

I whipped my head around to the voices.

"Let's get the honky!"

Heart hammering – I was the honky!

I had no time to count how many there were – and maybe my memory is faulty – but there seemed to be about fifty African American men running toward me, yelling and waving their fists. A two-by-four shattered the windshield. Consciously or unconsciously, I'd left enough space between my car and that in front to allow me to make a U-turn.

Ever since that day, I always leave enough room, and I try to tell Ellen and my daughters to do the same. Always give yourself an escape route.

I had one that day. I managed to get through the crowd, a few kids jumping out of the way as I plowed forward. I drove back to the psychiatrist's house, my hands shaking on the wheel. Even with all my pranks and antics, I'd never come this close to being badly hurt and possibly killed.

Years later, on the Martin Luther King holiday, I was sitting in an executive office on the top floor of a high-rise office building in Denver, consulting with the CEO of the Colorado public utility, when an announcement over the loudspeaker interrupted us: riots in Denver!

I started to sweat, a ball of anxiety gathering in my stomach and throat. *I think I'm having a flashback. I think this is what people with PTSD experience.*

In 1968, I took the actions I needed to, while stuffing my feelings deep, but they lived there inside me, erupting all those years later in that office with its plush carpeting and mahogany furniture.

I stayed two nights with my friend, the psychiatrist, before daring to venture back home again. A black man I considered a good friend, lived down the hall from my apartment. I called him before driving back and asked, "Do you think it's okay for me to come home?"

"Andy," he said. "Keep your white ass out of here."

I didn't know what to think. He'd never talked to me like that. Was he being friendly? Helpful? Warning me? Angry?

I stayed another night before returning. This time, I felt my fear. I parked, climbed the stairs, locked my door, loaded my .38, and turned on the television that was airing a segment about a nearby church where people were distributing goods and food for those whose homes had been burned.

It was time to take action. Sitting at home like a self-imposed prisoner wasn't doing me or anyone else any good. I drove to the church, hoping I could help. I parked my car a couple of blocks away, and walked into the church vestibule. White people stood behind a row of card tables doling out clothes, household items, and food. On the other side, receiving the goods, were black people.

A black man about my age stood in front of me. "Can I help?" he asked one of the organizers.

The white person said, "No. Thank you anyway."

I had one thought: *I don't want to have any part of an effort where white people are the only ones in the helper position and black people are only allowed to be recipients, even as the organizers are asking for help on television. This is so wrong.*

I turned, walked back out the doors, and headed up the street to my car. Coming toward me were two black men, one about twice my size. I was six feet and weighed about one-sixty or seventy. One of the two guys was about two inches taller and probably weighed about two-thirty. He was bare-chested and I'm pretty sure his muscles bulged. He looked like a weight-lifter. His friend was about my size and looked pretty tough too.

What the hell am I going to do now?

It took seconds for me to assess my escape routes: right? Left? Turn and run? My fear felt like a sickness inside me.

The space between us closed. What should I do? I was one lone white guy in a black neighborhood.

I felt my muscles coil. Time to run.

The big man smiled at me. "Hi, brother!"

Did I cry then? No. But today, the memory brings tears. I wish I could go back in time and ask him, "Why did you treat me like that after what happened?"

I tumbled from terror into relief, and then into gratitude.

I'll never forget the night Robert Kennedy was murdered in 1968. I was watching his celebration speech after winning the California presidential primary when I fell asleep. Then something woke me up and I found myself watching the live broadcast right after he was shot. His body was taken by train from California to Washington to be buried at Arlington cemetery.

The night his train arrived in Washington, I got on my motorcycle and followed the motorcade to Arlington. It was a dark night that was lit up by the flashing red lights of the convoy of vehicles. The next day fresh red roses lay on his newly dug grave. I still have that image engraved on my mind.

I remember wondering what the long-term impacts would be from the assassinations of President Kennedy, Reverend King, and now, Senator Robert Kennedy. I still wonder how different our country and world might be had these transformational men had a chance to lead us further.

CHAPTER 9

HARVARD

Because I had a uniform, I could fly free on military stand-by. I took advantage of that one day and flew home to Denver in my uniform. I also had a beard and long hair. My parents were waiting for me when I got off the plane and my father was furious.

He refused to walk with me down the airport concourse all the way to the car park. He didn't raise his voice – that wasn't his style. But his tone was brittle. "You are so fortunate not to be in Vietnam," he said. "But you're wearing a uniform and you're disgracing it when you have a beard and with your hair curling over your cap like that. It's not right."

I don't remember if he added that he was ashamed of me – possibly not. Still, his words shocked me. I think I understood him at the time – at least to some extent. Over the years, I've grasped his viewpoint and agitation more thoroughly. I've done a lot of things I regret, and I've acted in ways I should not have, but I've always had a shred of insight when I was wrong, even when I was being defensive.

Bottom line: my dad was right. I was in uniform and respect is important.

During the two years I worked at St. Elizabeths, it became increasingly clear to me that I wanted to continue my education and obtain my doctorate. I believed the advanced degree would give me more influence and credibility while also allowing me to contribute more meaningfully. I would also earn more money, and though that certainly mattered, it wasn't at the top of the list.

I applied to several doctoral programs, including Harvard's, remembering the advice I'd received from Archie Ward, the sociologist at St. Elizabeths Hospital. I also applied to the University of Pennsylvania, Berkley, and a handful of others, and received a gratifying number of acceptance packets, including from Berkley and Harvard.

Harvard! How could I pass that up? Still, I hesitated. In order to study for my doctorate, I would first have to enter their one-year master's program, then re-apply for my doctoral studies. Was I willing to take the risk that I might not be accepted – even if the risk was relatively small?

It was the late sixties and I decided to check out the University of Berkley California campus. It baked in the California sun, girls with books under their arms and flowers in their hair – the boys in bell-bottom pants and round sunglasses perched on the ends of their noses – used bookstores and tiny cafes with rickety tables spilling out on the crowded sidewalks – guitars strummed on every corner, often competing with a dreadlocked man on a soapbox protesting war, capitalism, and meat-eating faculty members.

It was tempting, but the offer from Harvard was too good to pass up, and I had a full scholarship. My four years of graduate school were paid for, including my tuition, books, and living expenses. Looking at the cost to attend college today, I realize how very fortunate I was. I stayed with a physician I'd met at St. Elizabeth's until I found a terrific little apartment in Cambridge not far from Harvard Square.

I was admitted into the School of Public Health, one of about a hundred in my class, eighty-five percent of whom were physicians studying for their MPH. I was in the department of behavioral sciences headed by the man Archie Ward had told me about – Alexander

Leighton, a world-renowned psychiatrist who had taught at Cornell before coming to Harvard.

He was a multi-faceted, multi-talented man who'd had previous appointments in the Cornell business school and the departments of anthropology, sociology, and psychiatry. He began doing original research in the 1940s – research that continues to this day.

He wrote numerous papers and books, including *The Governing of Men,* outlining his research at a Japanese internment camp in Arizona during World War Two. There had been an uprising at the camp. As a navy officer he was sent there to discover what was going on in that community. He had a breadth and depth of knowledge in the social sciences that allowed him to write his book with deep understanding of the situation. Certainly, it's the most comprehensive book I've read on the topic of governing people. It covers the principles of leadership and governance, relating to his diagnosis of how this particular community had arrived at a dysfunctional state. It also includes his recommendations for improving the conditions.

I found him a difficult man to relate to. Where I was fairly extroverted and wanted to make a personal connection with him, he was quiet, impersonal, and controlled, speaking softly and slowly. I didn't receive the feedback I needed from him and wasn't entirely sure where I stood. It bothered me enough that I actually felt like leaving the program. Fortunately, I saw a psychiatrist, who helped me a great deal. Toward the end of my first year, I also took a class in the Laboratory of Community Psychiatry, headed by Gerald Caplan, another well-known psychiatrist. My professor and psychiatrist, Ralph Hirschowitz, became a special mentor. My relationship with him served to balance my concerns in the Department of Behavioral Sciences.

The fact is, I was also a bit intimidated by Harvard, at least for the first couple of months. At the beginning of the semester, the entire class met in a large room where staff bombarded us with arcane facts about the degree we were studying for, and made sure to tell us how lucky we were to be in the program. I got the picture pretty quickly: the people talking to us were special because they were at Harvard and we were special because we'd been admitted and weren't we all just one amazing bunch of people. Yes, I was properly intimidated, which I gathered was their point, but I also thought, *boy, these people are really full of themselves.*

In fact, I wrote down my impressions: "The climate at Harvard is as follows – the students pretend to each other that the other is exceptionally bright. The faculty pretends to students that the students are exceptionally bright, and other faculty members are exceptionally bright, and finally pretend that students at Harvard are the equals of themselves. When everybody thinks they are a cut above the system, then you have described the climate at Harvard."

Most of my classes that first year were fascinating. Because my major was in behavioral sciences, I took a lot of classes with Leighton, a seriously interdisciplinary man who had worked with Margaret Mead, Clyde Kluckhohn, and other founders of cultural anthropology. But I studied with other amazing people who were prominent in their field: two cultural anthropologists, a sociologist, another psychiatrist, and Robert Benfari, an experimental psychologist with an MBA who later became my thesis advisor. It was a richly interdisciplinary department.

Biostatistics and epidemiology were tough that first year, even though I'd done good work in statistics previously. I simply didn't catch on to epidemiology as quickly as most of the physicians. But I achieved my master's at the end of the year and was accepted into the doctoral program. That's when my Harvard experience blossomed and bore fruit.

I was like a kid in a candy store: so much to learn! So much that interested, fascinated, and dazzled me! I intended to take full advantage of Harvard and the intellectual advantages it offered. I took classes, mainly with Leighton and the faculty in the department of behavioral sciences, in the School of Public Health, focused for the most part on his longitudinal study on Sterling County Nova Scotia (not the real name) that he began in the 1940s. His research involved people going door-to-door in the community interviewing the residents to determine if they had a psychological disorder. Based on the answers, he tried to determine how much disorder existed, what type it was, and where it existed within the community.

His hypothesis posited there would be more psychiatric disorder in what he called disintegrated communities that displayed a lack of leadership and communication and where people felt disconnected and without the power to improve their lives. This fit neatly with my understanding and interest in systems and context and how they affect people.

The effect of systems on people was a novel way of thinking at the time, especially in the forties when Leighton began the project. He had trained with Adolf Meyer, one of the most influential figures in psychiatry in the first half of the twentieth century. Meyer was president of the American Psychiatric Association in 1927–28 and rose to prominence as the first psychiatrist-in-chief of the Johns Hopkins Hospital. He was also one of the first psychiatrists to take a patient's environment into consideration.

Working at the St. Elizabeths Hospital in Washington DC, I'd become fascinated with family therapy, not surprisingly, given my interest in systems. Family therapy was started by a very few people, some of whom came from a Freudian background, and I read their books voraciously. I came to Harvard with a strong systems perspective that still informs what I do today when working with executives and organizations.

I took classes all over Harvard: in the School of Education from William Schofield, a psychologist who wrote *Psychotherapy: The Purchase of Friendship*; with Talcott Parsons, a sociologist of the classical tradition, best known for his social action theory; with George Homas, a sociologist whose research contributed greatly to the study of human interactions and social behavior; with Freed Bales, a social psychologist who pioneered the development of systematic methods of group observation and measurement of interaction processes; and with David McClelland, a world-renowned psychologist noted for his work on motivation need theory. McClelland made me a teaching fellow, which certainly bolstered my self-esteem. He posited that we were motivated by either a need for achievement, power, or affiliation. Each one of these men was recognized world-wide in his field.

I was so enthralled by the opportunities for learning, I audited several classes, just to soak up as much information as my mind could handle. In the class on organizational analysis, we read a book a week, each by an anthropologist or sociologist, and then wrote a review. Another resource in my smorgasbord was the Laboratory of Community Psychiatry, headed by Gerald Caplan, another world-renowned psychiatrist who developed preventative models for psychological dysfunction, such as crisis intervention and mental health consultation. He helped begin the community health center movement that would bring people out of institutions as soon as possible.

I took a class at the laboratory in family therapy from Ralph Hirschowitz, a psychiatrist from South Africa who worked in Israel during the Arab-Israeli war in 1949. He was a special man and I count myself fortunate that he took a liking to me and offered me a job. While I worked on my doctorate for three years. Ralph paid me to undertake three projects – one each year.

Thanks to him and the work I was doing for him, my confidence grew. Ralph was extroverted and showed great confidence in me, and I needed that because I still found Harvard fairly daunting.

Each year, he sent me out to a different catchment area in Massachusetts, gave me a psychiatrist to check in with, and told me to make a contribution to the area.

The first year, I decided to pursue my interest in discovering the factors that led to alcohol abuse. I spent a part of that year talking to people in the Metropolitan State Hospital due to alcohol abuse. At the end of the project, I wrote and published a paper in *The American Journal of Public Health.*

Based on that experience, where I learned that many residents at the hospital were either divorced or separated, I wanted to know, what is the relationship between dysfunction – in this case alcohol abuse – and marital breakdown? That became my project for the second year, fitting nicely with Ralph's directive to make a contribution in the area of mental health prevention.

With a judge's permission, I went to a probate court where people were getting divorced with the idea of creating a program that would help newly divorced or separated people cope with their loss and the dramatic changes in their lives. I believed that if I could help stabilize people and get them through this period with as little stress as possible, we could avert a psychological breakdown.

I discovered that Robert Weiss, a sociologist at the Laboratory of Community Psychiatry, had written a book on marital separation. His ideas dovetailed with mine. Ralph introduced me to him and I used his seminars as a springboard, sending a letter to everyone in that jurisdiction who filed for divorce or separation, inviting them to take part. The subjects covered included dealing with children, handling finances, dealing with your ex-spouse, dating – each seminar presented by a speaker and covering a different topic. The ten-minute lectures were followed by a discussion period.

I'm still proud of the work I did there and the results I achieved. The program went on for many years and may still be running. I wrote a paper on it, outlining the principles I used to develop it and how I embedded it in the system so it wouldn't depend on one person to manage it.

In addition to his academic duties, Ralph was also head of prevention for the state, meaning he worked to de-institutionalize large state hospitals. One of those institutions was the Foxborough State Hospital, historically known as the Massachusetts Hospital for Dipsomaniacs and Inebriates. My third-year project took me there.

I headed a team of people from the laboratory who were working with Ralph for a year to learn about community psychiatry. Our job was to consult with the mental hospital, and that boosted my confidence quite a bit more. All those on my team already had their doctorates. Morrie Schwartz, who was a sociology professor at Brandeis at the time and the first person to study a mental hospital as an organization, supervised our work every week. Years later, he became well known through the book, *Tuesdays with Morrie,* written by Mitch Albom, another of his students as Morrie was dying of ALS. I consulted with the CEO of the hospital while the others on the team met with different units in the institution, helping them consider how to move people out of the hospital more quickly, getting them more treatment and less custodial care.

Before starting on my dissertation, I had to do my oral exams in three areas: community and social psychiatry, organizational analysis, and applied behavioral sciences, the last one particularly important because it was defined as the application of psychology, psychiatry, sociology, and anthropology in creating change.

I was apprehensive about the oral exams – sitting all day with three designated professors, answering their questions, and doing it with a certain amount of aplomb. I was afraid I wouldn't pass. Happily, I did, and the professors were probably never aware of the sweat dripping down my back under my well-ironed shirt.

I wanted to write my dissertation on the question of what helps people in psychotherapy. A lot of ideas and theories existed, but not a lot of outcome studies. Where was the research on what helps and why it helps? I spent hours, days, and weeks hunched over long wooden tables, sorting through card catalogues, and moving between the stacks of that lofty library trying to do a review on the effects of psychotherapy.

I was naïve to think I could do my dissertation on that subject. It eventually became clear to me that if I was to get my doctorate, my dissertation would have to be on a piece of Leighton's work – that was what this department was all about.

My dissertation became a utilization study on Leighton's book, *A Sterling County Study,* a fictious name to preserve confidentiality about a location in Nova Scotia. I looked at people from the county survey who needed help, trying to understand why some accessed help while others didn't. I looked at factors like ethnic background, distance from a clinic, marital status, and other variables. Combining my background in social work and systems with Leighton's work, I strove to understand the impact of community organization. If you organize a community, you increase leadership, communication, and people's feelings of confidence. There wasn't then and still isn't now, a lot of research on the subject.

The research I did became an annotated bibliography of about ninety pages and an appendix to my dissertation. A few years later, I submitted it to a number of reputable publishers, one of whom said it was good, but needed to be longer to make it a worthwhile project for them. I wasn't willing to add "fluff" so I found a small publisher at Stanford who printed it.

My dissertation was a bit unusual. We were expected to write publishable papers. Mine was a publishable paper that I never published. It simply became part of Leighton's body of work.

Those years at Harvard weren't all about hitting the books. I dated, went to the beach, hiked in the mountains, camped, explored Boston, and spent hours browsing through the wonderful, musty stacks of books at the co-op bookstore in Harvard Square and the tucked-away little shops in Cambridge. I count those years as some of the most stimulating and exciting of my life. I also became aware of the importance of regular exercise to good psychological and physical health, and exercising became a regular part of my life.

CHAPTER 10

ELLEN

During my time at Harvard, I met Sara Ehrmann, a distant cousin who lived in Boston. Sara's mother was my maternal great-grandmother's sister. her husband, Herbert, got his undergraduate at Harvard and then graduated from Harvard Law School. He was a defense attorney for Sacco and Vanzetti, Italian immigrants and anarchists who were controversially convicted of murdering Alessandro Berardelli and Frederick Parmenter, a guard and a paymaster, during the April 15, 1920 armed robbery of the Slater and Morrill Shoe Company in Braintree, Massachusetts. Seven years later, they were executed.

By 1926, the case drew worldwide attention. As details of the trial and the men's suspected innocence became known, Sacco and Vanzetti became the center of one of the largest causes celebres in modern history.

Herbert wrote a book, *The Untried Case,* about the Morelli gang, who he thought had actually committed the murder – the case he wanted to put on trial but never could.

As a result of the Sacco and Vanzetti case, Sara became committed to abolishing capital punishment and played a large role in achieving that in Massachusetts. She became like another grandmother to me, one I found stimulating, smart, and caring. I would go to her house for dinner, feeling very much like we were family.

Herbert died the first year I was at Harvard, and Sara and I became even closer. I would take her shopping, and one time, I drove her to Norfolk prison. I remember walking through those forbidding metal gates behind this tiny grey-haired woman in her seventies, knowing that fragile as she appeared, it was wise not to mess with her.

She visited the prison regularly, talking to people who had life sentences and who were on death row, trying to understand their stories. She told me they needed to be accountable for what they did, but state sanctioned murder was not the answer. She had data showing that when there was an execution, more violence and murder occurred in the community where the execution took place and especially where publicity prevailed.

I went to an affair with her once where she was a dignitary of sorts. Someone introduced her to Eliot Richardson, the head of the Department of Health, Education, and Welfare in President Nixon's cabinet. I suspect she knew who he was, but when she was introduced, she said, "Eliot who?"

I recall that he was a pompous man and I suspect her aim was to let the air out of his ego just a bit.

Sara was indirectly responsible for introducing me to my future wife, and when we had our first child, we gave her Sara's name.

Sara fixed me up with a girl I dated once or twice. She was nice but there were no sparks. Then, during my last year at Harvard, driving home one night, I was stopped at a red light when the woman I had dated walked in front of my car. I honked my horn and she came over to my rolled-down window. "Come over for dinner!" she said.

I did, and she introduced me to one of her roommates, Ellen Wise. I was instantly enamored: a textbook case of love at first sight. She had bright blue eyes, smooth tanned skin, shining dark hair, and a wit that could easily match mine. I teased her and she gave back as good as she got. She sparkled. I can still see her sitting on the couch, her smile, quick-witted responses, and giggle disarming and tantalizing me.

We had Lipton onion burgers for dinner, and you have to be a certain age to appreciate a food fad that involved adding dry soup mix to ground meat.

I didn't care what those burgers tasted like. My attention wasn't on food. Ellen ticked all the boxes – cute, nice, funny, witty – and she was Jewish. Religion wasn't important to me, but when I saw the psychiatrist during my first year at Harvard, I realized that finding a Jewish woman to marry was more important than I'd thought.

I was dating another girl when I met Ellen, and Ellen had a serious boyfriend who was coming back from a few months in Europe. All of that paled in comparison to what was happening between us that evening. I knew she could be the one I'd been looking for, and I had been searching. I'd pick up a girl for a date and ask myself, "Could she be the one?" I knew almost instantly every time that the answer was no. I wanted to get married and have a family, but no one had ever made me feel like this. Ellen was the one.

On our first date, I decided to play it cool. I told her I'd pick her up at five and didn't arrive until after six because I didn't want her to know how much I liked her. A lot of guys did that, but it was a tactic that didn't fly with Ellen. She was sitting on the front porch with her roommates, drinking a gin and tonic, and she was righteously angry.

The truth is, I wasn't really being cool – I was afraid she'd reject me.

Luckily, she didn't.

Our relationship moved quickly. Ellen informally moved into my apartment after a few dates. I told my parents right away while Ellen never did give her parents the news. I recall a telephone conversation she had with them and though I could only hear Ellen's side, I had a solid sense of her father's words, "Of course, dad, Andy's going to walk me back to my apartment."

Living together with her took some getting used to for both of us. One legacy from dad was my notion about the right way to do things. One of our first conflicts involved cutting cheese on the countertop in my little kitchen. I cringed inwardly, afraid she would nick the countertop. I told her to stop, and not too kindly.

She said, "Andy, I'm cutting it on the countertop because your plates are plastic and if I scratch something, I'd rather it be their countertop than your plates." And that was the beginning of fifty years of interactions, all ending pretty much the same way.

But during those first six months or longer, I did everything I could to present the best me. I told her at the time, "I'm not usually this nice. I want you to know that."

I don't think the warning made any sort of impression. How could I be anything other than the me she saw every day? But I was aware that I was working at being kind, nice, witty, and loving Andy – and because I cared about her, it wasn't difficult. I was compassionate, compromising, listening, and genuinely interested. Ellen had no reason to suspect she was getting anyone different than who she was with. The more critical, judgmental Andy only surfaced later when I began to face the stress of a new job, new city, a big move, home hunting, and collaborating with another person after living alone for so many years.

Shortly after we met that summer in July, I drove to Denver. The night before I left, we were standing in the parking lot of her apartment, leaning on my car, gazing up at the stars, knowing we would miss each other. Ellen had baked a pan of brownies that'd I'd slipped under my car seat, overwhelmed with the realization that she cared for me enough after such a short time that she would do that for me.

That feeling lingered with me as I started my drive, and as I picked up a hitchhiker outside Boston. Those brownies held so much significance, I refused to share them.

Ellen flew to Denver a couple of weeks later. She was afraid of flying, but again, she cared enough to overcome that fear – and I was so happy to have her come out. In the week or so she was there, we stayed up all night talking a couple of times. And that's a hallmark of our relationship even today – we talk. Through all the ups and downs of the years, we have never run out of things to gab about. When times were hard for us, we always found a way to work it through, although not always promptly, which would have been ideal. As recently as the summer of 2023, we were sitting at our local pool, with our daughter, Becky, and her friends at another table. One of them looked over at us and asked Becky, "What do your parents talk about all the time?"

I was pleased with the recognition. Ellen and I can talk about each other, our relationship, other people, philosophy, current events – anything. It's the backbone of our relationship.

But my parents were concerned. What were we up to all night? Well, we were talking about the meaning of life, Ellen sitting on my bed, me sprawled on the floor, leaning back against her, both of us watching the dawn lighten the sky and spilling color into the world, turning the leaves on the old trees from charcoal to gray to olive and finally glittering green.

Ellen took a shower with the sunrise, emerging from the steamy bathroom with her hair in two long pigtails. She couldn't possibly have looked any cuter. We walked from the house to the nearby park where we sat on the grass still damp from morning dew, still talking about the meaning of life.

Maya Angelou said, "I've learned that people will forget what you said, people will forget what you did, but people will never forget how you made them feel."

When I think back on those early days with Ellen, I remember much more about how I felt than about the subjects we talked about or the things we did. With her I felt secure, loved, cared about, and excited, not just about what I had but also about what the future would bring. She was the way forward I'd always wanted.

At the time, I had a dark green 1969 Fiat Spider convertible. We drove it up to Rocky Mountain National Park on the highest paved road in North America and took a photo at the top that we later framed. Another day we drove into Grand Lake, getting out of the car late at night to look up at the star-studded sky, and I remember saying to Ellen, "Let's not lean on the car. We might scratch it."

Figure 6 Ellen and me in Rocky Mountain National Park 1972

Another foreshadowing of my obsessive, perfectionist nature.

Ellen finally flew back east to spend time with her parents in Connecticut. That's when Ellen phoned and told me Dirk, her old boyfriend, was coming home. I was standing in the kitchen, hung up the phone, and turned to my mom, telling her about my fears.

She sat down at the table. I believe she knew about the guilt Ellen was feeling – her own experience with meeting my dad had been so similar. "If you really love Ellen, you should get back in your car and get back to Boston as soon as you can," she said. "But don't do it unless you really love her. You have to be honest about this."

I took her advice, and packed and left the next morning, breaking speed limits all the way from Denver to Chicago where I made a brief stop at my best friend, Robbi's house. That night, he and his wife and I got pretty stoned – so stoned that at one a.m. I called Ellen, who was back at her apartment in Boston, just to hear her voice, waking her and her roommates. Ellen was not pleased. Then, for some unfathomable reason, I called my parents, who were also less than happy about being woken by a jangling telephone.

And suddenly, I sank into a deep depression – a pit so deep I could see no purpose in living. After all, I'd just pissed off the people I cared for most. I trudged to a city park, with Robbi's wife walking with me and talking me down.

The next day, my head clear, I hopped into my little Fiat and sped to Boston, hitting eighty or ninety on the Massachusetts Turnpike. My visions were all of Ellen – seeing her, holding her, having her rush into my arms. Pumped up on caffeine and excitement, I opened the door of my Cambridge apartment, and there was Ellen – asleep on my bed. Of course she was asleep – it was past midnight. But in my fantasy, she wasn't asleep. She was as excited to see me as I was to be with her.

Ellen had not conformed to how I thought she should be. That habit of expectations has haunted me all my life, especially with my daughter, Sara, who believes I've had images of who she should be rather than accepting her for who she is. And isn't that the same complaint I'd had about my father?

A couple of months later I started to get invitations for job interviews from various institutions in the U.S. and Canada. One night I talked to Ellen about the pros and cons of each offer. She said, "You don't need to include me in your decision-making because I won't be moving with you if we aren't married."

That was the kick in the pants I'd needed to start thinking seriously about asking her to marry me. To this day she insists it wasn't an ultimatum, although I like to tease her that it was.

When I began considering my future career, someone asked me, "Andy, what are you going to call yourself when you get your doctorate?"

I had no idea. With a master's and a doctorate, I was more than a social worker, but my doctorate wasn't in psychology, it was in behavioral sciences. I wasn't even considering becoming licensed as a psychologist, and it was an issue because it impacted the kind of job I was looking for. What did I want to do? Going into academics was a way to apply what I had learned, but I didn't want teaching to be my only focus. I also wanted to put my knowledge and experience to use by working with communities and people. I had an offer from Auburn University in Alabama. Living in and getting a sense of that deep south community interested me, although in retrospect I think I would have been miserable there.

I also had offers from St. Louis University and the University of Nevada in Reno. I interviewed at both and was tempted by the latter for its new program in behavioral sciences. But when I visited the University of British Columbia in Vancouver, there was no doubt where I wanted to be. Nothing compared to that beautiful city with its bays, inlets, mountains, and forests. And the job was perfect – a joint appointment as assistant professor in the School of Social Work, assistant professor in the Medical School

Department of Psychiatry, and the head of social work in the psychiatric hospital. It was everything I wanted with more applied work than academic.

I was completing my dissertation while Ellen was in the middle of a master's program for elementary school counselling. In the evenings and on weekends, she proofread and edited my dissertation. One night in December, we were sitting on the subway on our way home. I'd just accepted the job at UBC, and was talking about moving to Vancouver. In an off-the-cuff and somewhat impulsive way, I threw out, "I'm so grateful and thankful to you for spending so much time and doing such a good job editing my dissertation. Hey, maybe we ought to think about getting married."

And that was my best attempt at a romantic proposal.

So, we were thinking about getting married, although we weren't quite sure what that meant: were we engaged to get engaged? We called Ellen's parents first. Where were we going to live? Might Ellen leave the east coast and move to Denver? When I told my parents we were thinking about getting engaged, they said, "What does that really mean?"

Good point.

Ellen and I were married on June 3 at a Hilton Hotel in Hartford Connecticut. The huge windows let in a gentle breeze and gave us a view of beautiful Bushnell Park and the impressive Capitol. I stood at the altar, Robbi, my best man, standing just beside me – Ellen more beautiful than I had ever seen her in her white gown and long, lacy veil.

At the appropriate point in the ceremony, the Rabbi turned to me and said, "Do you take this woman to be your lawfully wedded wife?"

I choked, all my emotions rising into my throat. Impossible to speak. Not a word came out as I fought for control.

Silence.

Robbi told me later that he grew increasingly concerned and wondered if he should push me or maybe punch my shoulder as we used to do when we were kids. "Andy," he thought. "Have you changed your mind? What the hell are you doing?"

One last swallow and I finally managed to choke out, "I do."

And I did – truly and deeply, I did.

The day was a surreal blur. I remember shaking hands in the receiving line. There was a cocktail reception. Speeches? Probably. It felt like this momentous occasion was an event happening to someone else. I'd achieved my doctorate. I had just married the love of my life. I had a dream job waiting for me. It was almost too good. Was it really happening? Was it a dream?

It would have been wonderful to have been more present – but here we were, swept up in a sea of good fortune, and all we could do was ride the waves.

And just when I thought I was about to rise weightlessly into the sky, my buddies brought me down to earth – the buddies who had been plotting, possibly for years, to get back at me for the pranks I'd pulled on them. My father had given me a brand new Datsun 240Z – a dream of a car. Ellen and I left the reception. I walked over to the car and stopped in my tracks. Centerfold Playboy pictures obscured the front license plate. Tin cans hung from the undercarriage, criss-crossed streamers blocked the doors, Limburger cheese was stuffed down the gearshift knob, and rice and cheese down the defroster vents. The car stank for years. In fact, I don't think I ever got all the Limburger out. Sure, I'd had it coming, but that doesn't mean I didn't feel my feelings: anger at what they'd done to my brand new car, amazement and admiration for the fact they'd done it, helplessness because I didn't know what to do and knew I couldn't just drive away with the car in its current state, and appreciation that I had friends who cared enough to get so creative and go to so much trouble to completely prank me.

Figure 7 Decorated car at our wedding June 1973

My father-in-law, a sober and serious man, was in an apoplectic stupor, frantically tearing at the Playboy picture on the front license plate. Meanwhile, I sat in the driver's seat doing my best to mitigate the effects of stinky cheese. "You know," I said to Ellen, pointing to her father in front of the car, "This might be my one and only chance to get my father-in-law."

We drove away. Ten minutes later, I stopped at the first gas station we saw, so I could clean the car as best I could. We continued to Boston to a downtown hotel where we had booked a room. Surprisingly, it wasn't ready and we had to cool our heels in the bar until almost midnight.

Ellen had classes the next morning. I drove her to the campus and then met with Robbi and his wife to take them on a tourist circuit of the city. What I didn't know was that Ellen's class had been cancelled and she had to while away her first day of being a married lady completely on her own.

I graduated a week-and-a-half later, this time happily wearing my robe with the three stripes indicating I had achieved my doctorate. In the summer of 1970, when I attended my master's graduation, I had worn a suit with an armband as a protest against the war in Vietnam. About a third of the Harvard student body tangibly demonstrated their objections that day. My mother even marched with me in an anti-war rally. But on that hot summer day of 1973, I was in proper graduation dress, not quite believing I had actually done it – that after being a terrible student for so many years, I had come so far.

Figure 8 Harvard graduation with Ellen June 1973

My dad didn't say he was proud of me, but I knew he was. I have an image of him standing outside my apartment on the steaming sidewalk, holding my degree with a smile that went from one ear to the other. The memory still brings tears to my eyes. His approval and pride meant so much.

CHAPTER 11

VANCOUVER

Later that summer, we drove three thousand miles across the country to Vancouver to embrace our new life. Driving into town on a warm sunny day was an extension of the surrealistic experience I'd been living since my graduation and wedding. We headed along Marine Drive, lined with towering trees, in awe of the beautiful homes and well-tended gardens lined by cedar hedges and glorious rhododendron bushes with their leathery, dark green leaves. Ahead of us were the mountains of the north shore, houses climbing up the lower slopes. It was so unrealistically beautiful, it might have been a movie set. The sun threw diamonds off the water as we approached Kitsilano beach. It seemed that every owner of every house had been out that morning tending to their lawns and gardens, just in order to impress us.

We crashed on the floor of a Harvard friend's apartment right by the beach on West Second Avenue. Looking out from his windows at the beach, English Bay, and Stanley Park was bliss, and it didn't take us long to realize this was the perfect location to rent an apartment.

It should have been an idyllic time, but I was beginning to feel the stress of a new job. Was I really right for it? Would I do well? Was I up for it? Maybe I wouldn't meet their expectations. It was also Ellen's first time so far from home, and we had so much to do to get settled. We had to find a place to live, get a bank account and a telephone line and, most of all, familiarize ourselves with a new city and country. We knew no one except my Harvard friend. The stress meant my temper flared too easily and my best self was fading away. One day, Ellen and I had a disagreement about something and I lashed out.

Shock!

My regret was instant and lingers to this day. Lashing out was part of a cycle that went on far too long: me becoming impatient and angry, attack – and then the regret. *Andy, what are you doing? Why are you acting this way. Stop! This is horrible! This is not you. This is not who you want to be.*

I felt shame, embarrassment, confusion – why was I losing control? Why was I acting so horribly? I knew it was wrong but I was unable to control myself. Or was I able to exert control but chose not to? I opted to be impulsive, and that's a trait that has always been with me.

Even recently, on a trip to Banff, when I watched a couple of young guys cross a raging river using three poles as stepping stones, I simply had to cross the same way. Totally disregarding my age and the danger, and on sheer impulse, I stepped out. At one point, I almost fell. And then I had to recross on the way back. If I had fallen, I would have been gravely injured. I realized then, more than ever before, that my impulsiveness has gotten me into trouble.

Throughout my life, something would trigger me, and without thinking, I would act. In many instances, those actions were lashing out at the woman I loved, and I can never erase the shame or regret.

I had two offices at UBC – in the psychiatric hospital and in the school of social work. I still have my brass nameplates: Andrew L. Selig MSW ScD from the hospital and Dr. A.L. Selig from the School of Social Work. The latter was at the end of Point Grey Road beside the Museum of Anthropology. Gazing out my window I had a perfect view of impossibly tall cedars and lush gardens that would rival a tropical paradise.

Beautiful as it was, it took time for us to adjust. I had a new job to learn and make my own. Still, it was tougher for Ellen. She had no job and no close friends. Both of us had blithely moved to Vancouver without taking into account that even though Canada was a close neighbor, it was still a different country and we would have to make adjustments. Also, we had moved from the East Coast to the West where the culture was radically different.

And then there was the weather – the incessant Vancouver rain, just enough every fall, winter, and spring day to require the intermittent setting on the windshield wipers but never at quite the right speed. We stayed indoors far too often. With her typical wisdom, Ellen remarked one day, "This is just the way it is and if we're going to do stuff, we'll just have to do stuff and not let the rain stop us." And then she promptly bought an assortment of umbrellas in rainbow hues to brighten the grey days.

I may have felt a bit of trepidation about my new job, but mostly, I was excited. I inherited a small staff in the social work department but in a fairly short period of time, some left and I was able to hire my own people in the old and newly-created positions. I quickly became proud of them and the work they were doing. We changed their function in the hospital to one where they played a more direct role in the patients' care, and we embraced the importance of involving the family in treatment. At the same time, I became more caught up in teaching and supervising medical students doing various forms of family therapy.

To some extent, the feeling of everything being surreal continued to linger. "How could this be happening to me?" I wondered. In some ways, I still feel that at times. When I started my clinical practice in Denver, and later, my organizational consulting practice where I'd sit in fancy offices on plush leather couches, talking with CEOs of corporations, the thought would loom in my mind: "How can I be doing this work with these people at this level?"

The little kid who played pranks and got into trouble was alive and well and wondering how...

But my predominant feeling was excitement at having this ideal job. I met Dave Freeman at UBC. He had his doctorate in social work from the University of California and had competed with me for the job. I'd been chosen because the head of the Department of Psychiatry, who had made the decision along with the Dean of Social Work, had leaned heavily toward me. Dave was subsequently hired as an assistant professor at the School of Social Work.

We became close friends in one of those rare and beautiful relationships where we shared a strong professional connection while also genuinely liking each other. We had a lot in common, and not just professionally. Even our wives liked each other. We spent many long evenings talking over dinner, and during the week, David and I would talk over lunch. He was a gifted therapist who wrote several books on family therapy. I published a couple of articles in two of them.

It was a relationship I treasured until he died suddenly of a heart attack years later while on a bicycle trip in Europe.

Vancouver was a little behind the United States in terms of developing community health centers. But Milt Miller, the chairman of psychiatry, made a connection with the city authorities, and our department was designated to start The West Side Mental Health Center serving Kitsilano, Shaughnessy, Dunbar, and Kerrisdale. Miller named me the point guy for developing it and getting it up and running.

I started the organization from the ground up, hiring the people to staff it including a psychiatrist, the head of nursing, and the front-line people. I pondered the strategy of the place as well as the values and vision, knowing we would have to agree on them.

I felt strongly that our center should have a systems family orientation, identifying patients in the context of their families, whatever their status. I also stressed home visits with the idea that we could mitigate the hesitancy to get help if we were willing to see people in their territory.

I found a location and we got to work. With one exception, the experience was excellent – and even the "exception" worked out in time. If one of our patients needed to be hospitalized, we sent them to the Health Sciences Center Psychiatric Hospital. Given my training and education, I knew a good deal at this point about community health and felt strongly that we should use just one inpatient unit for our referrals. I wanted a continuity of care, and if we used one unit, we could build relationships with the staff. Our patients would get better care and could likely be released more quickly.

The hospital psychiatrist, who had worked for the World Health Organization, disagreed with my approach. I pushed hard to follow my vision and succeeded, but not without ruffling his feathers. I heard about it at a meeting with Milt Miller. While he gave me positive feedback about the work I was doing and what my team was accomplishing, he also said, "But Andy, you have one flaw – and it's a big one. You don't understand the needs of fifty-year-old men."

I don't think I fully understood at the time what he was trying to convey, but his words are ones I have reflected on over the years. I was thirty then – and he was right. I believe he meant that I should listen more to the experience and possibly the wisdom of older people. I should weigh their thoughts and ideas and perhaps push my own ideas a little less. I was American with a degree from Harvard and I had ideas about how things should be done. I was also from the East Coast, transplanted to the Canadian West Coast, which tended to be more laid-back. Maybe I was being perceived as being a bit arrogant by people who were less overtly aggressive? Certainly, I doubt I had enough genuine appreciation for the perspectives of people who had more experience than me.

Miller gave me terrific feedback that I believe helped me grow as a person. I know when I was in my fifties and sixties and supervising younger people, I felt about them the way that psychiatrist must have felt about me.

At the time, I was determined to have my way. I said to Ellen, "One unit is just the right way to do it. I'm going to go to Milt's office and tell him I'm not going to do this anymore unless they do it my way."

Ellen said, "Wait, Andy. Let's think this through."

Those were words I would hear many times over the years. Ellen would calm me down and help me be more thoughtful and objective. There's a theory that's been around a long time saying that the man is the more logical partner in a relationship while the woman is more emotional. That has certainly not been the case in my marriage. And from my clinical practice experience, I'm even more convinced that stereotype is not true. In our partnership, I've definitely been the overreactive, impulsive one while Ellen has been far more rational. However, when working with clients, I've always been able to focus completely on them and their challenges, maintaining my rationality and objectivity.

I didn't go to Milt's office with my ultimatum.

During that early time in Vancouver, I had the idea of tracking how things worked in the in-patient unit at the hospital using a computerized system. When patients left the hospital, they would fill out a form commenting on their experience, which would allow us to evaluate how good a job we were doing. It was a revolutionary project manned by volunteers and social work staff.

We developed a questionnaire and got it computerized. I wrote a paper on the results. If I remember correctly, we discovered that patients did better when their families were involved in treatment – and that was what I was all about. It has always been a large part of my perspective that people should be seen in the context of their social, community, and cultural relationships and that it's critically important to take this into account when helping them move in better directions. We found that when family members were involved, people got out of the hospital sooner and were more satisfied with the care they received.

At that time, I also started my own practice, the Behavioral Science Consulting Service, doing some clinical work and consulting to organizations. The biggest assignment I undertook involved flying to Vancouver Island each week where I met with leaders in the social welfare department dealing with topics like management and leadership. The flight in a small single engine plane that provided amazing views of the mountains, bays, lakes, and ocean was a highlight.

In some ways I felt like a big frog in a small pond, delivering talks in various settings across Canada. My presentations included a paper on building a community mental health team at a Canadian Public Health Association meeting in St. John's, Newfoundland, consulting on the power of and need for interdisciplinary teams in Regina, Saskatchewan, delivering social work services in a comprehensive health care delivery system in Edmonton, Alberta, and evaluation of community mental health in Toronto.

CHAPTER 12

A DAUGHTER

Ellen found a job in our first year in Vancouver as an assistant director in a volunteer coordination center. I believe that was a big relief for her, but her real happiness came a few months later when she applied for a job as an elementary school counselor for four schools in Surrey, a municipality just south of Vancouver. Within twenty-four hours, she received a call-back from the head of counselling, hiring her without even requiring an interview. The reason? Ellen was a Smith College undergraduate. The head's wife had received her MSW at Smith. He said, "Anybody who went to Smith College in Massachusetts is competent and bright."

Ellen loved the job and did exceptionally well at it.

Living at 2171 West 2nd Avenue, just three blocks from the beach, meant Ellen and I had a great jogging route. I'd started jogging in Boston about 1970 when I grasped the fact that regular exercise was important to health and well-being. We would run from our apartment to the beach, along the beach, around the planetarium and all the way back, our senses filled with the ocean, Grouse Mountain, salt air, mewing seagulls, and warm raindrops.

Our life began to settle. I was less stressed at work and. Ellen was happy with hers. Through a family connection we met an older couple who were lovely, kind, and gracious. They invited us for dinner shortly after we arrived, making us feel much more at home. On one occasion they introduced us to an American couple, Bob and Jane Cancro, who became close friends for life. Bob was doing his residency in orthopedic surgery at Vancouver General Hospital, having previously worked on the Crow Indian reservation in Montana for the Public Health Service. Jane was a public health nurse.

Vancouver had an especially big attraction for me. I'd been interested in birds of prey since I was a young boy. I remember driving in dad's convertible with the top down, trying to spot birds of prey flying overhead or perched on fence posts and utility poles. In Vancouver, all we had to do was drive a few miles north along Howe Sound to Squamish where bald eagles congregated every fall, often in the thousands as they followed the spawning salmon.

Ellen would bring the newspaper or a book while I did my best to get the "perfect" photo of a bald eagle. I'd be out there for hours, stalking the birds. 'Why isn't that picture good enough?" Ellen would ask. "Why do you need to go back for more?"

I couldn't explain what the perfect eagle picture looked like, but I was determined to get it. I doubt I ever did, because no matter how brilliant it was, there had to be one that was even better. This striving for "more" has probably been another hallmark of my approach to life with both positive and negative consequences. I took hundreds and hundreds of photos, sometimes of so many eagles in a tree there were almost more birds than leaves.

We drove to Whistler once with Bob and Jane and another couple and we all got stoned in the hot tub before lying down in the snow and laughing hysterically at the stars.

When Ellen got pregnant, we moved to a rental house at 2710 Waterloo Street. A baby! I was incredibly excited. I'd always wanted to be a dad – and here it was about to happen! We wanted to use the Leboyer method, also known as birth without violence, where the room is dimly lit and quiet and the baby is laid on the mother's stomach, allowing the infant to listen to a heartbeat familiar from the womb.

Unfortunately, we couldn't find a doctor to provide that service. However, we had an excellent general practitioner and attended childbirth preparation classes where the men practiced helping their partners concentrate on their breathing. To this day, Ellen likes to remind me that I may have taken my job too seriously.

The instructor asked us to squeeze our partners' Achilles tendon to create a bit of pain, allowing the women to practice their breathing through the discomfort. Ellen insists I squeezed hard – too hard – and sometimes without warning. In my defense, I wanted to prepare her.

"Andy!" she would say. "That hurts!"

"I know! But childbirth is going to hurt too."

Were the other husbands doing it too lightly? Maybe. Not me. I'd also bend down and squeeze her Achilles tendon at various times during the day, surprising her, and hoping it would prepare her for what was to come. She was not always impressed.

On July 17, 1976, Ellen did a beautiful job of bringing Sara into the world, and I like to think that my pain infliction played some small part in that.

Our first night home, Sara fell asleep after Ellen nursed her, but then woke up an hour or so later crying inconsolably. We didn't know what to do. The nurses at the hospital had instructed us to only feed her every four hours. At two a.m., worried as only first-time parents could be, we called the La Leche League for advice, not knowing the phone number would wake up a volunteer and her husband. She assured us that's what she had signed up for and gave us "permission" to feed Sara whenever she seemed to need it, at least while the three of us were getting adjusted to our new lives. Then Ellen's parents arrived soon after our return home. Her mother was especially helpful.

I don't think my feet touched the ground for the first year of Sara's life. I was high as a kite, totally enamored with her. I would sneak into her room at night and crawl under her crib with a recorder just to tape her breathing and her baby coos. I was utterly smitten. I envied the intimacy Ellen had with nursing, wishing I could do the same. I wanted to cuddle her and hold her. The Snuggli baby carrier was wonderful – I could strap it on and hold her close to my chest just under my chin, breathing in her baby sweetness.

From the moment Sara was born, her eyes were open, taking in this mysterious, glorious world. I would walk down the street with her nestled close to me pointing out trees, birds, buildings, cars, clouds. In retrospect, I think I overstimulated her. She was already tuned in and sensitive to her environment and I may have done too much.

When she cried at night, I'd get up, change her diaper, and bring her to Ellen to nurse. She was a colicky baby who was hard to soothe, and like so many new parents, we wanted to do everything perfectly – which is probably why so many of us screw up the first time. Ellen refused to buy processed sugar and salt laced baby food, making her own instead from pureed fresh fruits and vegetables, freezing individual portions in ice cube trays.

No matter how many mistakes we made, being a dad to Sara was one of the highlights of my life. Soon after she was born, we brought her to meet my parents in Denver. Coming into the driveway, I spotted a Canadian flag my dad had found and displayed in front of the house to welcome us home.

Among the many causes my mother volunteered for was the Children's Hospital. She loved babies, holding the desperately ill ones as they were dying because she didn't think babies should die alone. She was the first and only volunteer in the newborn center to be allowed to hold babies. She had masses of experience with them and knew a lot about them.

We hoped she could help in our struggles with Sara who would cry and cry inconsolably almost every time we put her down for a nap or to bed at night. My mother's advice was to put her on a schedule and let her cry. We took her advice, but it wasn't easy. I remember sitting in my parent's house after putting Sara down, hearing her crying and crying, our hearts breaking, believing we simply had to get her on a schedule. We still don't know if it was the right thing to do.

Living in Vancouver was probably good for us because we were far away from the influence of our families and had to find our own way. But my "not best" side continued to show up – at least for another fifteen years. By "not best," I mean my impatience, leaping to judgment, and insistence on doing things my way. I was aware when I was behaving badly and not being the person I aspired to be, but I justified those times by telling myself it was how I was raised. The excuses I used changed nothing.

CHAPTER 13

DENVER AND A NEW JOB

After four beautiful years in Vancouver, we moved back to Denver. It wasn't an easy decision, but now that we had a baby, we wanted to be closer to family. The Dean of the School of Social Work and Milt, the Chair of Psychiatry, were more than gracious, wishing me luck in my new endeavors, but also offering me a lifeline. "We're going to keep your job open. If it doesn't work, we want you to come back."

We'd agreed that we wanted to live in an integrated area in Denver, and we particularly wanted Sara to grow up in a muticultural and multi-racial world, so we bought a house in Park Hill, an older neighborhood, near the area where I grew up.

Buying a house was a significant step for us. We'd saved all Ellen's earnings in Vancouver, living strictly and frugally on my income. We had fourteen thousand dollars for a down payment on a sixty-three thousand dollar home. It wasn't big or grand – just a modest two-story brick house, but it was perfect for our small family.

I started my job search before making the move, and found one as clinical director of the Adams County Mental Health Center that saw me reporting directly to the CEO as the number two person.

I was responsible for about ninety clinicians and four sub-offices – a bigger job than anything I'd previously undertaken. The Adams

County Mental Health Center was considered one of the best in the country that was mentioned in at least one or more books published by the National Institute of Mental Health as an example of a top flight mental health center that was connected with the community and other agencies, as well as offering auxiliary services.

Unfortunately, that was in its heyday. When I came on board, the glow was fading. The psychiatrist who had founded the center and the previous clinical director, both of whom had put it on the map, had left. The current CEO and I were filling big shoes.

Compared to Vancouver, my office was nothing to get excited about. And unfortunately, my job also fell short in comparison. The center was in a low-income suburb occupying a small building. My office had a view of concrete walks and nondescript office blocks. Even the people around me seemed dour in comparison to my former colleagues.

When we moved, I had no idea of the shock the change would bring. But I found my feet, got to know the people, and did my best to meet my responsibilities. Within weeks, I met Larry, a psychologist on one of my teams, and we became friends, playing racquetball and chatting over the occasional lunch. Each of the four-sub-offices I was responsible for was headed by a leader, and when one of them resigned, I had to hire or promote someone to fill the position. Larry was one of the applicants.

I didn't pick him – and that turned out to be a big problem because he was certain I'd choose him. In retrospect, I question the authenticity of our friendship, but I also mistrust my own motivations for my ultimate choice. I liked Larry, but I didn't think he'd be the best person to lead the office. At the same time, I was also afraid of giving him the position in case it was seen as favoritism.

Regardless of motivations, I got pushback from a lot of people. I think most agreed with my decision, but there were others who were firmly in Larry's camp, and he was furious. Why hadn't I chosen him? What was I thinking? My explanations fell on deaf ears. I'd assumed Larry would be upset, but I hadn't been prepared for his full-on resentment.

Then I compounded the problem with good but naïve intentions. At about this same time, the CEO handed in his resignation, opening up his position. I was his logical replacement, but the idea of doing his job or even that of acting CEO overwhelmed me.

I called the Board Chair. "You know," I said. "Larry is really upset with me. I don't think he was the right guy to head the sub-office, but I think you should consider making him the temporary CEO."

Again, I admit to a secondary motive. It wasn't just that I didn't want the job, I also wanted to appease Larry. That was naïve. In retrospect again, and everything makes so much more sense when you look back, I should have discussed it with Ellen. She has always been my ground and my voice of good judgment. Not talking to her at length was probably my biggest mistake in the whole sorry affair.

The board followed through on my advice and appointed Larry the CEO. On his first day, he called me into his office. I sat down in front of his desk – a vast clean surface punctuated by a yellow legal pad, a list covering the first two pages.

I had a strong sense of a set-up.

He handed me the pad. On it he'd written forty-eight demands I was expected to meet. I remember one in particular: develop a volunteer program. That one, along with most of the others, had an exacting timeline. Not possible, I thought, especially the volunteer program.

So I did the only reasonable thing I could be expected to do. I rolled up the yellow sheets and pointed them at Larry. "Larry," I said, "Shove these up your fucking ass!"

He fired me for insubordination.

I'd made a poor decision with my recommendation to the board, and now that I've spent forty some years consulting to CEOs, boards of directors, and executives, I've discovered how common choices like this are at the highest levels of some of our biggest corporations.

It amazes me that our companies are as successful as they are given how irrational and chaotic the decision-making process often is. Fortunately, more good decisions are made than bad, and few as bad as the one I made.

I came home that day to the house we'd just bought and to the mortgage we had to pay, and to the fact I was the sole breadwinner and said, "Ellen, I just got fired."

"What?"

Now what? Well, what about my Vancouver lifeline? But just two weeks previously, I'd written to the dean and Milt, telling them I was nicely settled into my new job and they didn't have to keep my old position open any longer. We could also let go of my landed immigrant status.

About half the people at the mental health center supported me when I left. "Andy should not have been fired," they said. "He's been off to a good start and he's done a good job."

I don't know what the other half said, but the bottom line was that after eight months, I didn't want to stay anyway. I'd never been able to stop comparing my position to Vancouver with its wonderful job, location, and people. I suspect I had a slightly negative attitude the entire time I was there.

And then, after all the smoke had cleared, I made a good decision. I realized that in spite of my success in Vancouver, being a leader in a situation rife with politics and loaded with the challenges and difficulties that came with that territory, wasn't what I was best suited for. I was inclined to be too impulsive and to take things personally. I was better suited to helping others think through their issues and decisions rather than doing it myself.

Fortunately, the board gave me three month's severance, and that gave me some breathing room. Since arriving back in Denver, I'd been doing what I'd learned so well from my dad – meeting interesting people and being curious about what they did. I'd reached out to people working in the mental health field. Today it's called networking. My dad called it, "making contacts." It worked for him and for me because we were genuinely interested in other people and their concerns. My networking paid off.

As a result of the contacts I'd made at the University of Colorado Medical School's Department of Psychiatry, I had a job there within a week or so after being fired. But my new position didn't begin for another two weeks, so Ellen and I flew to San Diego with Sara for a terrific beach vacation with friends we'd made in Vancouver. He'd been a Marine who saw combat in Vietnam. Naturally, I was full of questions for him, wanting to understand some of his experiences. They must have been horrible because despite my sincere efforts, he didn't want to talk much about them.

I thought my new job, back in academia, was a good fit. It felt safer and perhaps more familiar. In that setting, I believed the gap between my capabilities and what I needed to accomplish wasn't wide enough to be overwhelming.

In the mental health center, I'd been intimidated by the thought of being a leader in a much bigger, more complex, and challenging environment than the one I'd been in previously. Academics was well within my comfort zone. My posting as assistant professor of psychiatry was at the John F. Kennedy Child Development Center where I was head of the department of social work with three or four staff under me. The Child Development Center was a tertiary referral source for families whose children had some sort of handicapping condition. We were an interdisciplinary team consisting of an occupational therapist, physical therapist, developmental pediatrician, psychologist, nutritionist, dentist, and a social worker (me) whose job it was to assess and train others to evaluate and understand the family dynamics inherent in their situation, and recommend ways to maximize how the family functioned and dealt with their child.

After our assessments, we would come together as a team to talk about, analyze, and ideally, synthesize our findings and make recommendations to the family.

It more closely resembled the work I'd been doing in Vancouver and had far less stress than the work at the mental health center. I stayed in the job four years. When we had turnover, I hired people whose thinking approximated mine. Some aspects of the job suited me exceptionally well. I supervised University of Denver social work students and met people in pediatrics and family practice. One pediatrician brought me in to teach pediatric residents about family dynamics to help them understand how families work. I did the same for the faculty and residents in the family medicine department.

That role was particularly fulfilling because the knowledge I had was unique, and once again, I had a bit of that same sense I'd had in Canada – the feeling of being a specialist who was giving physicians valuable perspectives that would help their patients and families. I was also having fun, working with residents and helping them take into consideration the family aspects of issues they were dealing with.

My contact in the pediatrics department became the chair of the American Academy of Pediatrics and a leader in the United States in his discipline.

When our team at the Child Development Center met to talk about the cases, I consistently felt tension between myself and the chief psychologist, an extremely capable guy who went on to have a stellar academic career, doing cutting edge research on learning disabilities. Our interactions often had respectful disagreements. I felt he put too much emphasis on what was going on with the child and I suspect he thought I was giving too much weight to the family dynamics.

One day, we decided to do therapy with a family together. During the process, we realized we were much more closely attuned in our methods and thinking when we worked hands-on than we were with our theories. I've never forgotten that. It was a great lesson in being careful about making assumptions and being too competitive and adversarial, when finding what we have in common with others both personally and professionally can be so much more productive.

CHAPTER 14

ANOTHER DAUGHTER

Becky was born June 15, 1979. The pregnancy was very different from Ellen's first, and turned me more toward nature rather than nurture. Even in utero, Sara and Becky were polar opposites. Sara had moved around constantly. You'd think she was trying to escape or play a rousing game of soccer. Becky was quiet and calm. As adults, both are bright and capable, but while Sara is more ambitious and sensitive like me, Becky is more like Ellen, taking life as it comes.

Toward the end of the pregnancy, Becky moved even less. Ellen's doctor became concerned and sent her to the hospital for non-stress and then stress tests, both of which were inconclusive. He then decided to keep Ellen in the hospital overnight so they could continue to monitor the baby's heart rate. The doctors considered inducing labor in the morning but it became a moot point, as Ellen began labor on her own at about 10:30 p.m. and delivered Becky about an hour and a half later! Luckily, she was in the hospital because the labor went so quickly. If she'd been home, I doubt we would have made it to the hospital in time.

Becky's birth was nothing like Sara's. The doctor informed us that Becky had passed meconium in the womb, meconium being a baby's first poop, which usually occurs after birth. When it happens in the womb, it can highlight important medical concerns because it may be a sign of fetal distress.

We were worried, not only because of the meconium, but also because of her decreasing level of activity. But she came into the world and was fine. Meanwhile, I was concerned because I didn't think I could love another baby – or anyone at all for that matter – the way I loved Sara.

Long before Becky's birth, I confided as much to my mother, who told me a story she had read or heard. Love, she said, was like a burning candle. The candle can burn brightly, full of love, and you can use that candle to light another. The flame will be just as big and just as bright. The second won't diminish the flame of the first. It was a great metaphor, and it was exactly what happened. I fell in love with Becky, just as I had with Sara – and both loves burned equally bright and strong. Becky was a wonderful, special, and precious baby. And now I had two girls I was deeply and irrevocably connected to.

Becky was about three weeks old when the physical therapist I was working with said, "Andy, all our students see kids with problems. Would you bring little Becky in so they can see a normal baby?"

"Sure," I said. "I'd be happy to bring her in."

We did, and I went on with my work. The next day I had a note in my box from the therapist saying, "Andy, we need to talk."

That's never a good phrase.

We went to lunch. "I've got bad news," she said. "We were with Becky yesterday and we think she may have cerebral palsy. Or she may be intellectually disabled, but she definitely has problems. You should feel lucky that we caught it so early so we can help you with early interventions."

My world fell apart.

I went home to tell Ellen. The news shattered her. When we pulled ourselves together, we talked to the physical therapist and the occupational therapist. How had they arrived at their conclusions? Two things: she turned herself over from her stomach to her back, which is a milestone task, but the occupational therapist said she did it in the wrong way. Also, they spun her around in some way, which made her cry, which indicated something was wrong.

We were completely devastated. But they were ready to help us, just as they helped other families at the center. They gave Ellen exercises to do with Becky, and had her come in a couple of times a week to work with them, but after a while – perhaps a couple of months, Ellen said, "You know Andy, I don't like this. I don't feel like I can relate to Becky normally. I feel likc I'm more focused on what is wrong with our daughter and fixing that rather than on just loving, nursing, and caring for her. I really don't want to do this anymore."

We had also been reading about infant development and Ellen felt pretty strongly that Becky was still within the normal range of development.

"You can't stop doing this," I said. "Do you know how many kids we see whose parents denied the problems and didn't do anything and then they come to us and its past the critical stage – and it's too late for us to do anything? I really want you to keep doing this."

The tension between us was palpable. We finally saw a well-known child development psychiatrist in the medical school who had published work on early childhood development. We told him our issues and our questions. Was this something to be concerned about? What should we be doing?"

"Let her play on the floor," he said, watching her closely.

"She's fine," he said. "Stop worrying about her."

We wanted another opinion and visited a developmental pediatrician with his own practice. His opinion? "Stop worrying. She's fine."

And we did.

And they were right.

During the years I was at the University of Colorado Medical School, I gave a lecture on family dynamics to medical students in a course on psychiatry. I used my family as the case study, talking about how a diagnosis affects family dynamics. There was tension between Ellen and me about how to handle things, and Sara was acting out because she wasn't getting the attention she needed.

Our worries about Becky were affecting all of us. My mother stepped in and tried to give Sara extra attention because she could see how the situation was affecting her. It was a great professional study, showing how one thing creates a ripple effect through an entire family.

I gave the lecture for fifteen years, standing up in front of a hundred and twenty or more people using my personal example until the last couple of years when I found myself beginning to tear up. I believe it was because I had left my practice at that time to do consulting and was losing my clinical calluses. When I started to tell my story, I felt like I was reliving that time in our lives, feeling again all that trauma, fear, and uncertainty. I finally said to the teacher, "I love doing this but I just can't anymore. I'm embarrassing myself and I'm probably embarrassing you and watering down the message I'm trying to get across."

Figure 9 Sara, me, and Becky around 1985

CHAPTER 15

PRIVATE PRACTICE

The head of the Child Development Center became an advocate for me, helping me get grants and assisting with publishing papers. Along with the chair of psychiatry, he supported me in getting promoted to associate professor, which meant a lot. You had to publish a certain number of papers and have a national reputation, as well as doing clinical work and work in the community.

The promotion was exciting, but at the same time, I'd had enough of that world. Academia had its share of politics, and I wasn't interested in engaging. Staying to become a full professor didn't seem worth the effort. I wanted to test myself in another way. What could I do on my own, in my own clinical practice?

I needed a license to practice, and passing the Clinical Social Work license exam was the first step. For the oral exam, I was asked what my theoretical orientation was, and then I was challenged to answer questions about clinical cases. The problem was my systems orientation did not match up with the questions I was asked, which were based on a Freudian framework. I told them I could answer their questions within the Freudian framework, but since that wasn't my primary approach, I thought I should be able to respond to the questions as I saw fit. They passed me. Several years later, I also took the Psychology Licensing exam, passed it, and became a Supervisor for Marriage and Family Therapists.

Through teaching, I'd met a lot of residents who were now in pediatrics or family practice, who I could use as referral sources for starting my own practice. The head of the Child Development Center, graciously allowed me to work half time while I set up shop on my own. I found a family practitioner in a practice in the hospital near the medical school who rented me a small office in her basement. It had no windows, but it was mine and I filled it with second-hand furniture from the hospital and thrift shops.

I got referrals from the family doctor I rented from. That was a start. Then I leaned on the lessons I'd learned when I was ten, selling Christmas decorations door-to-door. I called internists, family practitioners, and pediatricians. I sent them my resume and took them out to lunch. "I'm starting a practice," I said. "I'm interested in what kind of psycho-social problems you see in your practice. Just as a way to get to know me and how I think, and hopefully to trust me and think I could be helpful to your people, if there are psycho-social issues, call me, and maybe I could be helpful by giving you some ideas of how you could deal with them. Hopefully that will open the door to you referring them to me."

Some took me at my word and started referring people to me.

It was an exciting time for me professionally. I had my own office. My degrees were framed and up on the wall. I had my business cards. I was a licensed psychologist, a licensed social worker, and a licensed and approved supervisor with the American Association of Family Therapists, certifications and credentials that meant a lot at the time.

Other people with practices started coming to me for supervision, paying me by the hour for my work. After about six months, I stopped working at the Child Development Center, focusing full-time on my own practice. A year later, I left the basement office and rented a larger space with windows looking west at the majestic Rocky Mountains!

Feeling pleased and excited, I renovated my new space, creating a waiting room, a room with a two-way mirror where I could supervise those I was training or where my trainees could watch me, and an office for me in the back where I saw my clients. I bought a couch, chairs, and a desk. I could sit in my office and look west to the mountains, and think, "How on earth did little Andy Selig arrive here with his own practice?"

I doubled my salary from $40,000 to about $80,000. With the mortgage payments and two children, we had been just getting by, unable to save money. Now we could finally feel more secure and begin to save.

Having my own practice felt like a trajectory I'd been on since I was selling Christmas decorations and magazines door to door. It combined my interest in meeting and knowing other people with an inclination toward entrepreneurship. My destiny was in my own hands. I was aware of that almost immediately on an intellectual level, but when I caught up with that knowledge emotionally, I genuinely began to feel the joy of what I was doing.

If I wanted something to happen – if I wanted to get ahead or try something new – it was all up to me. No one else.

I suppose I was following in my father's footsteps, or, more accurately, in his self-sufficient mindset. He occasionally wrote poems, and one that sticks in my memory is one he wrote when Ellen and I got married that spoke of his pride in me and the idea that my fate was in my own hands.

With great pride we send this check
To a son who works with great effect
We really we weren't sure, at the start
Just how far you'd get in doing your part
We're proud and pleased to be some part
Of your contribution to humanity and art
Your selection of a lovely mate

Insures our hope of both your fate
Our greatest wish to both of you
Is one only you can make come true
With love, good health, and weather fair
You've got it licked, you lucky pair.

Those words and thoughts applied even more strongly now that I had my own practice. From now on, it was up to me to create the life I wanted. While the thought was a bit scary, it was also strongly energizing.

I have a memory of those early days when I was still in the basement of the doctor's practice in the hospital. One of my father's friends, who was a Yale graduate and quite wealthy, was parked in the hospital driveway when I came out. If there was a longer conversation that led up to his words, I don't recall it – but I can still hear him say, "I always knew you had it in you."

Those words meant I was being seen and I believe I was beginning to see myself the same way, and I was excited to discover what I could do – how high I could reach.

My reach was good. People came to me, I got referrals, and my practice thrived. It did better than my family life. While I can recall events related to my career, my personal life is more vague. I was deeply focused on my work, putting all my capabilities into making sure I did well.

CHAPTER 16

FAMILY MEMORIES

Ellen and my daughters were deeply important to me. I don't believe I ever missed a soccer game. Both girls were good athletes and I loved watching them on the field. In addition to playing soccer, Sara was an excellent swimmer. Becky was an All City Soccer player, and both were involved in *Odyssey of the Mind*, an academic after-school program centered on creative projects supervised by a couple of adults. I attended preparatory sessions and the ensuing competitions.

Ellen and I also wanted to make family memories and took trips to many parts of the country. Sadly, they didn't always work out the way I wanted them to. Due to frequent family conflicts, Sara and Becky don't have the fond memories we wanted to give them.

From my perspective, Sara and I occasionally had special times together despite our challenging relationship, in which neither of us wanted to acquiesce to the other in our frequent power struggles.

The one thing I'd wanted to do differently from my dad was show my children that I was interested in what they were thinking and feeling – and I didn't succeed, particularly with Sara.

Ellen and I clashed over parenting. I felt Ellen was too lenient, particularly with Sara, who had a strong personality. I thought Ellen should put more limits on her behavior while she thought – and rightfully so – that I was too tough, too demanding, and too angry. And then, my toughness escalated because I thought I had to counteract Ellen's permissiveness. The pattern had negative effects for all of us.

The turning point came as Ellen was driving me to the airport one day when she said, "I love you, but if you don't control your impatience, anger, judgmentalism, and criticalness, I'm leaving you."

Ellen believes she did not preface her statement with, "I love you." Perhaps I invented those words to soften the blow they had on my heart.

I knew she was right, and I realized then that I needed to do something and stop rationalizing my behavior. I finally looked in the mirror and told myself, "If you want to keep your marriage, Selig, and if you want to be the kind of person you say you want to be and who you think you are, you'd better be that person. You can't think you are someone when that's not who you are."

From that point, I started to seriously look at what I needed to do to become more patient and compassionate. I wanted to save my marriage and be the dad I'd always wanted to be. It was a slow and difficult process that has taken many years. But that incident strengthened my belief that if you want to stay in a relationship with someone, you have to pay attention to it. I've always believed that if a person changes, their relationships will change as well. That has been my professional mantra and it was strongly reinforced by my personal experience. Had it not been for Ellen drawing a line, I don't think I would have changed. The shock of her words made me see more clearly, not who I thought I was, but who I actually was. It was the incentive I'd needed to make the changes I'd always known I had to make, but had for so long rationalized, denied, and put off. I saw it all: the source of my regret and my guilt, and the shame over not being able to control myself effectively. It took time, but eventually I felt reassured when Ellen expressed how impressed she was at my commitment to making these necessary changes and how successful I was in my efforts.

In later years, I talked to dad almost every day. He was always careful not to push too hard when he had opinions about what I was doing. More than once, he said, "Aren't you being a little tough on Sara?"

Sometimes I agreed with him, but usually I would say, "Yes but…" And I had my reasons or justifications. In retrospect, I wish he had been less subtle. I think his words might have registered more. During my one therapy session with Sara she said that I never saw her or recognized her enough.

It was the same issue I'd had with my father growing up. I'd repeated a pattern even though I'd consciously vowed, even before she was born, that I wanted to know Sara's feelings. I wanted her to be able to talk to me about her thoughts and emotions. I wanted to be the kind of father I'd wanted my dad to be. That was my big goal and I screwed up. Why? How was that possible when I wanted it so badly?

I had a core belief that I wasn't being recognized as I should be. And I was afraid of rejection. I think I was at least partly motivated to act badly as a test. If Ellen really loved me… she would… what? Put up with me? Tell me I was right? Do it my way? I think my thought was more that she would keep loving me in spite of how I acted. If she didn't reject me when I acted badly, it would prove that she really cared about me. That wasn't a conscious thought at the time, but it was certainly what was going on.

Until she reached her breaking point, Ellen did exactly that – tried to focus on the positives and make things work in spite of my poor behavior. Even when she didn't feel she was wrong, she would apologize. And I wouldn't relent, staying in my huff of anger until Ellen put her foot down. "Andy, that's it. I'm not doing any more. I've apologized, I've tried to move past this. That's it. Enough!"

And then I would finally turn around. That was my pattern – our pattern. It wasn't until Ellen stood up to me that I realized I had to stop acting like a jerk.

I'm sure that part of my being a jerk – and I don't use this as an excuse – was the time and the society I grew up in. America, and pretty much all of the Western World, functioned as a patriarchy. But being a male, I was unaware of that dynamic, or perhaps I didn't think it applied to me. What I did know was that I wanted to be seen the way my dad was regarded. I could probably count on the fingers of one hand the number of times he raised his voice. He wasn't an angry man. He had a quiet, commanding way of getting your attention and gaining respect. I think he was more internally driven, and not so affected by how others saw him.

I wanted to live up to his standards. In my role as a father, I still compare myself to my dad. My daughters and Mary's two daughters all looked up to him. I wanted that. I wanted to be seen like him.

Even more to the point, I wanted to be seen.

I still want to be seen.

And recognized.

It's been with me all my life – this feeling that I wasn't recognized in the way I wanted to be. But as much as I want to be recognized and seen, I do things to prevent it.

I want to be seen as a caring, sensitive, compassionate person who tries to make things better for others. I also hope to be seen as someone who is competent and bright. I want to be someone people want to be around because they feel better just being with me. I want to be someone others can connect with deeply, someone they can talk with freely and in depth.

Some say that if you want to be it, it's because you are it.

I hope I am the way I want to be seen and recognized. I believe Ellen sees that side of me. I would like my children to experience me that way but I don't think they do. I have close friends who do, despite my failings.

Ellen especially, knows my shortcomings, and she can still see me this way. I suppose my failings make me human, and humans make mistakes, have warts, and are sometimes jerks.

So, all the fond family memories we'd hoped to create on our vacations, didn't play out the way we'd wanted them to. I don't think either of the girls recall those times with joy.

My own memory is more forgiving. In fact, I remember our vacations with a lot of fondness. And I had fun. I think Ellen did too. We drove to California and the Grand Canyon and flew to the East Coast where we visited Ellen's family and spent time on the beach. We all remember a beach vacation on Cape Cod where we dug a huge hole, big enough for me to stand in without being able to look over the edge – and I was six feet tall.

That hole became the big beach attraction. Adults and kids all up and down the shore came to sit or play in the hole. There was even water in the bottom because we'd dug down so far.

We also went on several beach vacations with my parents and my sister and her family to Florida and once to Mexico.

A couple of times we rented a sailboat, even though I didn't know how to sail. How hard could it be? One time we were on the gulf coast in Florida. I had my daughters and two nieces on the boat and was doing pretty well until the wind died while we were still a fair distance from the beach. My only option was to jump into the water, grip the bolt rope between my teeth, and do the breaststroke, tugging the boat behind me.

Another time, Becky and I were on a rented sailboat in an inlet, which was too tame for my liking. I wanted to be out on the ocean. Once out in open water, the current started pushing us out farther and farther, and I couldn't control the boat. Becky, who was about ten, sensed my fear as I realized the peril of our situation.

"I want mommy!" She wailed.

"I want mommy too!"

We still laugh about that. But we weren't laughing at the time. I was genuinely concerned for our safety. Then I spotted a couple of men on a pier – a pier that was getting smaller by the minute.

"Help!" I yelled. "Help!"

A short time later, a couple of men – probably the two I had shouted at – motored out to us. They were not happy. Who was this idiot who knew nothing about sailing, but was getting into trouble with a ten-year-old on board?

I didn't blame them one bit for getting angry, and I was immeasurably grateful when they threw us a rope and pulled us back to shore.

Not long after that, Becky and I had another adventure. During the winter, when I was a kid, I'd sneak up behind a car at a stop sign, grab the back bumper, and get an exciting ride in the snow until I decided to peel off. Knowing that Becky was an adventurous ten-year-old, I drove with her into the Colorado mountains and attached a rope to a sled and the back bumper of our 1994 International Scout, long enough see her and keep the sled from sliding into the back. I drove slowly up the snowy jeep trail, and it was great fun until I tried to turn around. The Scout slid and became wedged with its front wheel partly off the edge of an overhang. After failing to pry the truck loose, I told Becky to get her toys. We were walking back to town. On the way down we ran into a couple of men who installed commercial air conditioning systems. They had winches in their truck and got us moving again. Becky remembers to this day how scared she was. I remember it as a special time I shared with her.

CHAPTER 17

FAMILY AND CAREER

As my parents got older, I became more attentive to them. They'd set that example when I was growing up and my mother and dad had lovingly helped her elderly parents. Dad looked up to his father-in-law, similar to the way he'd looked up to his grandfather who'd started with nothing and made something of himself.

Dad was also kind and caring to his mom, writing a letter to her every Sunday night. Both parents modelled attentiveness. But that wasn't the only reason I looked after them more and more. I loved them and wanted to be there for them. Dad and I talked almost every night. I drove them to doctor appointments, and helped with things around the house like climbing up on the roof to clean the gutters. I also helped with his rental apartments that he managed himself. I changed filters on furnaces, fixed humidifiers, changed leaky washers and faucets, and looked after anything else that needed doing. Along the way, I learned how to be a passably good handyman, which often meant that if you didn't know how to do something, you had to figure out how to figure it out.

But dad, being the perfectionist he was, was always looking over my shoulder to make sure I was doing it "right." I had mixed feelings about that. While I enjoyed being with him, I could also get a bit aggravated by the supervision. I remember standing on the roof of his house.

"Andy, are you sure you got all the leaves at the corner by the downspout?"

"Yes, dad."

"Are you sure it's clean now?"

"Yes, I'm sure."

"Let's put the hose down to make sure."

Whatever we did together, it had to be done right.

I loved him anyway, always. When I was working at the JFK Child Development Center at the University of Colorado Medical School, just a few blocks from my parents' house, I often had lunch with him. I enjoyed those noon-times, but dad never let up on me. Couched in a joke – but not really a joke – he would comment about how much I ate and how much it cost to feed me. When he was in his nineties I brought him some jelly beans because he really liked them. I came into his room once, walked over to his dresser, and took a couple of his jelly beans, popping them into my mouth. He got pretty annoyed about that. Those were his jelly beans!

When I was in my fifties and he was in his eighties, we drove from Denver to Taos in the maroon '67 Ford Fairlane convertible that used to be his and that I still own. We left southern Colorado and entered New Mexico, the wind blowing, the sun sinking like a giant red basketball in the desert. We climbed the high desert, the wind beginning to bite with chilly teeth. "Can we put the top up?" I asked.

My father chuckled, "No, Andy, we don't need the top up."

Figure 10 My dad and me in Taos, NM 1998

In the 1920s, he spent a number of summers there, hanging out with friends whose family, the Illfields, had a long history in New Mexico and were quite wealthy. He drove around in their Cadillac, went horseback riding with them, and met a lot of the now famous art community. He loved Taos so much, he and my mother even had their honeymoon there.

On one of our two trips to Taos, I asked him again about his growing-up years. He brushed off any questions that probed deep. "You know, Andy," he said. "I'm just a matter-of-fact guy."

I think my dad was always afraid I'd get lazy if he didn't poke me just a bit. And maybe he was right to an extent. There were times I tried to skate by. In order to get my bachelor's degree, I had to study a language. I wasn't interested in learning Spanish and I was about to fail, so I went to the teacher and lied to her, telling her I wouldn't get into dental school if I didn't pass the class. Of course, I had no intention of going to dental school. But she gave me a D to allow me to pass. Instead of studying, I'd used my social skills to get by – and sometimes I used them to get out of things too.

That said, I never tried to get out of things that interested me and that I cared about. All my life, I told myself the story that I was lazy. Maybe that story wasn't entirely true.

My practice kept growing as I continued to meet more physicians in the community and developed more referral sources. Over the next four years, people I saw also began to refer their friends to me. One day, a pediatric neurologist I'd worked with at the Child Development Center who had gone into a pediatric neurology practice said, "Andy, I want to give you some feedback. Some of the people I refer to you, come back and tell me you're really helpful to them but you tell them they don't need to come back as often as they feel they want to – that you kind of push them away before they feel ready for that."

His words were important and stuck with me. I have always wanted to err on the side of moving people on sooner rather than later if I felt they were ready. I never wanted to be perceived as someone who was trying to add more billing hours. Being ethical and fair are two of my highest values. The feedback I got from Larry was valuable because it made me think about where I was drawing the line. Was I doing it in the right place? While I always wanted people to think they were getting at least a little more from me than they were paying for, perhaps I was taking it too far. I hoped not. My overriding goal was to help and make a difference.

I'd often leave work late, but even when I was home, I'd be on the phone with my clients setting up appointments or following up, just wanting to know how they were doing.

One night, I was talking to a guy calling from a phone booth who had a loaded .45 in his hand, ready to kill himself. My focus was laser-sharp on only one thing: talk him down. Just then, Ellen came into my office. I waved her away. My world consisted of one man in a phone booth.

On the edge of my vision and awareness, I noticed her grab my clinical practice check-book and write something in it. When I hung up, with the man thankfully still alive, I turned to her in frustration to explain that I was trying to save a life! What was going on? The check Ellen had written was made out to Andrew Selig.

She apologized, but said, "The only way I'm going to get to talk to you is if I buy some of your time."

I will never forget that.

To be fair, she had no idea of the urgency of the call, but she was right. I was neglecting her and my kids. Instead of giving them the attention they needed, I was putting my focus on my clients and my practice.

One of the eye-opening experiences I had as a practicing psychologist was doing "ride-alongs" on an eight-hour shift with the police. They made me keenly aware of how difficult a cop's job was, and how they have to make life and death decisions in a split second. Several experiences stand out. One was getting a call about a shooting and spin-tailing the police car out of the station, lights flashing and siren wailing, to get to the location. On the way, the officer showed me how to release the shotgun in case it became necessary. Another time, we were called to a domestic disturbance call, considered the most dangerous by the police. The officer went into the house while I remained in the car, but after a few minutes he came out. "Doc, can you come in and talk with somebody?"

A teenage girl was crouched in the corner of a room, shaking and traumatized. Cautiously, I entered and talked to her, and I do believe I was able to help.

CHAPTER 18

CORPORATE LIFE

In 1985/86, things were starting to change in the mental health field. Insurance companies were questioning the way I was billing, making reimbursement more difficult. I used a limited number of diagnostic categories, usually depression and anxiety disorder, because I had no great faith in labelling someone with a specific diagnosis. I've never seen a good, strong link between a diagnosis and the methods I used to help people.

Insurance companies would look at my submissions and ask, "With this diagnosis, why aren't you seeing the person weekly?"

I tended to tailor sessions to peoples' needs. I might see them once a month or every two weeks. I cared about doing what they needed rather than what the insurance companies wanted or even what was general accepted practice. Dealing with the big conglomerates got tougher and tougher and was beginning to affect the way I wanted to practice. If I was working with a couple or family, I had to name one person as the patient, and that didn't sit well with me.

Even today, there is still a gap between what insurance companies need and what I think is the right thing to do for the client and their family.

In my days at the Child Development Center, I'd met Kevin Smith (not his real name), another psychologist who started his own firm of management and organizational psychologists. We'd briefly discussed the idea of me joining him, but though I was flattered by the invitation, my own practice was growing and I wasn't interested.

Now I was. Kevin's firm, Smith & Company (not the real name), employed a small stable of psychologists who consulted with CEOs and leaders of corporations and businesses in order to make them more productive and successful by helping people at the top be the best leaders they could be, and by helping the management team work together as seamlessly as possible. Making assessments of potential new hires was also essential. I'd be starting at the bottom, taking an income cut of about forty percent. I estimated it would take three years to get back to what I had been earning in my practice.

The decision was agonizing, and the money wasn't even the toughest part of the equation. My practice was doing well. It was special. I was making a difference in people's lives. I had no one else to answer to and I ran it the way I wanted to. The choice to leave and join Smith was so stressful it took a physical toll on me. I developed back pain so bad, I was in bed taking valium for most of two weeks.

I kept working, dictating reports that I would write up later. On one occasion, I thought I'd done a masterful job, only to have Ellen look it over and wonder what I was thinking. Clearly, I hadn't been thinking; I'd been buzzing on valium.

After still more painful pondering, I accepted Kevin's offer. I just couldn't jump through the hoops the insurance companies were holding out in front of me. But money was going to be tight, especially for the first year. My salary was scheduled to go up to fifty-five thousand in my second year and seventy-two thousand after that. But in my first year, I wasn't making a contribution. I had no clients of my own, and essentially, I was learning the ropes.

I got off to a bad start. Shortly after joining the firm, Ellen and I joined the other men and their wives for dinner at a Moroccan restaurant. I believe the men were making comments about me joining the firm. I was instantly put off by their pretentiousness and arrogance. I said, "I'm really happy to be joining the firm, and I hope I can bring some humility to it."

My statement probably set the tone for the next ten years, particularly in my relationship with Kevin. My colleagues didn't take well to the words I'd blurted out. But that was so "Andy" – impetuous and not thinking of the consequences. Or maybe I was thinking about the consequences and was willing to accept them because I thought what I was saying was right. And while it was a rocky start, I think I would have been unhappy regardless. I'm sure the stress of working there and the discontent I felt affected every area of my life.

I never felt I fit with some of my colleagues, but more people came on board during those years, including a couple of women I liked and enjoyed working with. I was flattered that they called me "one of the women" and invited me a couple of times to their all-women lunches.

As for my male colleagues. – the way they talked about our clients was almost always condescending. How did they come to the conclusion that they were somehow better than this roster of pretty impressive people? We worked with CEOs of multi-million dollar corporations and brilliant entrepreneurs who were generally a good deal older and with far more experience in business. None of us had overcome the obstacles many of them had in order to climb the corporate ladder.

I remember a meeting with the founder and CEO of one of the first cable companies in the United States, and one of the ten largest at the time. He was smart, brilliant, and eccentric. With an eye to developing more business with him, my two colleagues out-and-out lied about the firm's experience. I was shocked. *They're telling Glenn we've done stuff we've never done!*

That was just wrong.

Shortly after I started with the firm, two colleagues came to my house. One of them, a friend from before I joined, started going through my closet, which was full of brown and beige sport coats, some with leather patches on the elbows.

"All this has to go," he said. "You can't wear any of this. You have to get suits – blue and grey – no patches on the elbows. You're no longer some professor or therapist. You're going to be meeting with executives. You have to get a whole new wardrobe."

I went to a men's store and told the salesman what I needed and walked out with suits in shades of blue and grey.

To add to the stress of starting a new job, in 1986, we moved into a bigger house. I dragged my heels when Ellen suggested it, mainly because I didn't like to spend money. I was raised with the value that you spend money only on things you really need and you put money aside for the future. Ellen prevailed, as I think she usually does, and also as usual, I thanked her because she was right.

On a happier note, we also got a dog. Dori was an Australian Shepherd puppy, who immediately became a part of our family. She was smart, loyal, loving, and, of course, the best dog ever. In the mornings, she would bring in the newspaper and on hikes, she would herd us along the trail, nipping at our ankles if we were lagging too far behind – by her standards, of course. She died in October 2004, at age seventeen, suffering from arthritis, held close by the people she'd adored all her life, and who had unconditionally loved her back.

I'd been with the firm about a month when I flew to Buffalo, N.Y. with a colleague to consult with a company that manufactured large coffee-grinding machines. On our first day, we interviewed the senior management team, asking a lot of questions and engaging them in a discussion about how things worked in the company and what they saw as the challenges in their particular areas as well as the company as a whole. From that foundation, we could proceed with leadership and organizational development, which is now called coaching.

We asked questions like:

What's working?

What isn't working?

How are decisions made?

How is the CEO leading?

What are your challenges?

What are the issues and opportunities?

After eight or nine hours interviewing people on the first day, I couldn't sleep. I was excited, so revved-up and so mentally immersed in the puzzle that I couldn't stop weighing everything we'd heard about the dynamics of the company and the people. It was like trying to solve the puzzle of a family's underlying currents but multiplied ten times. There were more people and far more complex relationships and issues – all of that layered on top of the challenges any business faces.

I finally got up at three or four in the morning, knowing I wouldn't fall asleep. I walked the dark city streets, navigating from the pooling of light from one lamppost to another. I was utterly stimulated, trying to understand and make sense of what we had to deal with.

On our last night, we had dinner with the CEO. My colleague was smart and he knew it. In other words, he was painfully full of himself. At one point, the CEO turned to him and said, "You know, you're really a pompous ass."

Internally, I gave the CEO a standing ovation.

My colleague simply shrugged and said, "You're right. I am."

I have a need to be recognized and to contribute – it's basic to who I am. At the firm, I never felt seen for who I was or for what I brought to it. If I made a suggestion about making any small change, like tweaking how we did assessments, I was largely ignored. But I wasn't a raw recruit devoid of valuable experience. When I had my clinical practice, a couple of physicians and business owners would ask me to come in and help with their staff. Some of the course work

I did at Harvard and the consulting I did to the state hospital was very much in line with what we were doing. But my suggestions were always downplayed.

I was never a good writer and whenever I turned in a report, my colleagues would drown it in red ink. If I made suggestions about writing shorter reports so that we could charge a little less, they'd say, "Selig, you're just trying to water things down because you don't like writing reports and do a crap job of it."

True, I didn't like writing them and I did a less than stellar job of it, but my point was that we could save the client money and develop a stronger relationship because of it.

Kevin was adamant that no one could do this work on their own, so we also went out in pairs. Okay, two pairs of eyes and brains were probably good, but I'm not sure I bought into that as a necessity for producing good work. The problem was that we were charging twice as much as I felt we needed to, and I thought we were ripping our clients off.

I suspect one of Kevin's motives in insisting we had to work in teams, was to keep us from opening our own shops in the belief we couldn't do it alone.

For ten years, I was never free of stress, and I was never happy. I contemplated going back to my practice often, especially in the early days. But then I was once again facing the issue of insurance companies and the knowledge that the situation would only get more untenable with the years. I also believed that if I could do this work and become good at it, I would eventually make a lot more money, learn a great deal about business and industry, and help improve the lives of many people working in organizations.

In 1985, right before I started working with Smith & Company, Ellen enrolled in the MBA program at the University of Denver, graduating in 1990. While I was happy for her, I also resisted her decision. Tuition was expensive, and I didn't understand her motivation.

"Why do you want to do this?" I asked.

"I haven't been able to get a job as an elementary school counselor because schools are moving away from having them," she said. "I'd like to start the MBA program and see if I like it as a possibility of moving into a new field. And the University of Denver program has a part-time daytime option, so for the most part I'll be able to be home when the kids are home and still be able to do most of the household things I do now. I just want to try it."

Her answer didn't satisfy me. It didn't make sense, especially because I was taking a big pay cut. Regardless of what I thought, she went ahead and got her MBA.

A big concern was finances, but I admit that I also felt threatened and intimidated by her new role that would require me to step up more than I had been.

After graduating in 1990, she couldn't find a part-time job as she had hoped, so she accepted a full-time market research job with a company that provided drug, disease, and toxicology databases to healthcare professionals and patients. But she found that doing a great job while keeping up with all her duties at home too stressful.

We had a pretty traditional marriage. I was the breadwinner; Ellen looked after the kids and the house. Sure, I helped clean up the dishes, but basically, I worked outside the home and Ellen did the domestic chores. I still expected her to do everything she'd done before when she was home full time or in school part-time. I offered to do more of the shopping and cooking, but I was going to do it my way: big batches of food that we could eat for three of four days. Ellen wanted variety, especially for the kids. Because I wasn't about to do it her way, Ellen kept doing the cooking.

It was too much for her, so she asked her employer to put her on part-time. They agreed, but shortly after, eliminated her position.

Maybe I could have done more, but I wanted to do it my way and Ellen didn't push too hard. Looking back, I'm not proud of my attitude. But at the same time, I admired her intelligence, curiosity, and capabilities. I was impressed that she was challenging herself, especially because she didn't see herself as someone who put herself to the test.

As is normal with large organizations, Ellen was not given "two weeks' notice." She was told to pack her desk under the watchful eyes of a security guard, and then escorted from the building. Being a person of high integrity, she went out of her way to leave the center with all the information they needed about the projects she was working on. In her view, she was being meek and compliant – and I think she regrets that. But someone like Ellen will do what is right, regardless of the circumstances.

After that, she started her own business doing market research projects. Over the years, she also devoted her time to helping me with my reports.

Meanwhile, Sara and I were still at loggerheads, butting heads over control issues. Her backpack was the symbol of our struggles. I wanted it in her room. She left it in the kitchen. Such a small thing, and yet it loomed so large to both of us because it represented the line we continued to draw in the sand.

"Sara, get your backpack out of the kitchen!"

"Sara, go to your room!"

To this day, she's resentful about that, and I regret how I handled it.

Becky, who was three years younger, would observe our struggles, and one day, after Sara had stormed out of the room, asked, "Am I going to be like that when I'm a teenager?"

I found the work with Smith & Co. intimidating for a long time, but I wanted to grow and push my boundaries, expanding my comfort zone until I no longer felt awed when I walked into a CEOs corner office with its original artwork, plush leather sofas, and floor-to-ceiling windows overlooking the city. I wanted to challenge myself – that's really who I am.

I remember sitting in one of these massive designer offices one time, thinking, *what is Andy screw-up Selig doing sitting in here with these guys? How can I add value to a sixty-year-old who has worked his way to the top – to CEO of Public Service Colorado?*

That was the day one of the first Martin Luther King Day marches was taking place in Denver. Over the internal speakers came a public announcement telling us a riot was taking place on Colfax Avenue. In an instant, I was back in Washington, trying to get home while my neighborhood exploded in violence. I started sweating and shaking, unable to control my body or emotions. I was scared. I could be killed!

I had never experienced PTSD, but there was no mistaking what this was.

In time, the work with corporations became more satisfying but I still missed the intimacy and connection I'd had with my clients, especially when we were talking about the relationships that were important to them.

But I was convinced that the work I was doing with the firm would give me a better future. It was also fascinating work. I learned how industries and businesses work, from banking and hi-tech to entrepreneurships, family enterprises, health care, and much more. Over the years, with the firm and later on my own, I worked with several of the major telecommunications giants, gold mining corporations, manufacturing companies, internet companies, and others. I also worked with start-ups getting their footing in a garage or basement. The learning curve was intriguing, and kept me interested – that and the excitement of solving problems so convoluted, they resembled a Gordian knot.

And then, after untangling the knot, I had the job of giving the clients feedback in a way that was realistic, honest, reflected what I'd heard, and included my judgment and experience. I had to do that accurately and in a way that added genuine value. I also had to deal with a host of contentious issues, usually involving personality clashes.

To do that honestly and constructively was a challenge and a great reward. It was more complicated than working with families, but the most intricate situations were family businesses that came with a stew of company and family dynamics completely intertwined.

It still blows me away that I can interview a couple of people and develop a hypothesis, then interview a third and discover it's something else altogether. But then I'll talk to a fourth or fifth or sixth person, and by the time I've sat with ten people, I'm shaking my head, only to discover that my initial hypothesis was fairly accurate. I am constantly reminded how complex it is to get people to work together harmoniously – and how hard it is not to jump to conclusions and hang on to them rather than keeping an open mind. Sometimes, stubbornly hanging on to an opinion is the easy thing to do, but not the most helpful professionally or personally.

In spite of my negative views of some of my colleagues, I think all of us in the firm wanted the same thing – to give value to our clients.

In 1996, or just before, I started thinking seriously about leaving the firm. I'd pondered it quite a lot over ten years, but near the end, those thoughts became strong considerations. Ellen and I had discussed it, and she told me I had her full support. She had faith I would find success in whatever I chose to do. Still, I'd held back because I'd been afraid I couldn't develop my own client list. After ten years of hearing, "You can't do this work on your own," I think I'd begun to believe it. Sometimes repetition can be absorbed as truth.

The first turning point came when Kevin bought a building and charged the firm rent, setting a non-negotiable rate. I looked into it, discovering the rent he was demanding was exorbitant.

The second and deciding factor was when Kevin changed my employment contract, making it much harder to leave the firm and do the work on my own. I knew that if I signed, I would be indenturing myself – and I was already miserable – had been for ten years. Suddenly, I was so sure of my direction, I just told Kevin, "I'm leaving."

What a relief! It scared the hell out of me, but it was also a massive weight off my back.

Then something wonderful happened – almost every client I'd worked with said, "Selig – we're going with you. You've been the guy all along."

On my life's list of events to be grateful for, that one ranks near the top. I'd been intimidated, especially because I did the work differently than my colleagues: I was more personal. I cared. Apparently, my clients had noticed, and liked my approach.

I stayed true to my contract. For two years, I paid Smith twenty percent of everything I billed. I still have a trophy Ellen gave me on the exact day those two years were up: Congratulations! You did it!

CHAPTER 19

SELIG & ASSOCIATES

When I started my own consulting firm, Selig & Associates, I had many of the same feelings I'd experienced when I began my clinical practice: a combination of fear and worry that I wouldn't be successful while also being deeply grateful that my clients had followed me and that I'd make it if I worked hard enough.

Also, failure was not an option. That might have been something my dad would have said, and his attitude continued to influence me. I was going to do what I had to do to make it work: set goals, do a good job, and never give up.

Coupled with the intensity and pressure of my new practice was the excitement of the challenge.

Here I go again! Can I do it again?

Yes, I could. Unlike many others, I had a leg up to start with. I had clients and contacts from Smith & Company. Over the years, people have come to me for advice and mentoring on setting up their own similar practices, and I've told them that starting from scratch is different from what I did.

My work also involved traveling, an aspect I found exciting, stimulating, and exhausting. I'd work from early in the morning until late at night, sometimes interviewing as many as ten people each day, and then often having dinner afterwards with the CEO. In the interviews I had multiple goals: to assess each executive I talked with, understand how the senior team was working, and decipher the major challenges the organization as a whole faced.

I worked long hours – not as long as I had in my clinical practice, but the consulting work required a good many more written reports. Doing an individual assessment for development work or even an individual assessment of a candidate for a senior position in a company required a fair bit of writing, and, of course, I'd always found that intimidating.

Once again, I was blessed that Ellen had my back. She backstopped me so many times, both personally and professionally – I think too much so at times, and not for my sake, but for hers. I don't think I could have done a lot of what I did without her.

She had grown up to assume the role she took with me. She came from a musical family. Her mother could probably have been a professional pianist. Ellen has perfect pitch and played viola in the high school orchestra. It was her mother who encouraged her to take up the viola rather than the violin, because there are fewer viola players than violin players and she would have less competition. Her mother believed that number two was an excellent position.

While I was raised to be competitive and strive to be number one, Ellen grew up learning to be a good girl, take care of her family, make it her top priority, and to understand that success meant finding and marrying a nice Jewish boy with a good education.

I've often thought – and told Ellen as much – that if she'd been raised like I was, we'd never have married because she wouldn't have put up with me. She would have played the violin, and done it with great skill.

Unlike my earlier years, I don't have a lot of detailed, accurate memories of my personal or even professional life during my time with Smith & Company, or afterwards, with my new consulting practice. It doesn't follow a tidy, sequential order, and I don't know why not.

Was it stress?

When I left academia and opened my clinical practice, and now again, starting my consulting firm, I felt like my back was against the wall. I needed to bring in business, and I had to grow my practice and make it thrive. I was pre-occupied. My clients were my main focus, and professionally, that was the right place to put my attention. But it also meant I was less focused on my family than I should have been. Sara was already in college, but Becky was still in high school and subjected to the manifestations of my stress.

I think stress and striving brought out my tendencies toward perfection and control while also making me too quick to anger if I felt things were going the wrong way or that I didn't have enough control over a situation. Wrongly, and regrettably, I showed more patience and tolerance in my professional than in my personal life. On the occasions when I shared personal experiences, in hopes they would be helpful to a client, most said they were shocked given how they experienced me professionally.

CHAPTER 20

ADVENTURES

After Sara graduated high school, she took a gap year in Israel with *The Year Course in Israel* through *Young Judaea*. Along with other parents, Ellen, Becky, and I visited her for about two weeks during Christmas and New Year's. I experienced that trip as a turning point because it was the first time I felt proud to be Jewish. Seeing what the Israelis had done was inspiring, and I was deeply impressed with who they were. I hadn't even realized the extent to which I carried stereotypical images of them that I'd probably borne all my life, partly shaped by my family. For the first time, claiming my heritage made me feel more congruent.

I was fascinated by everything I saw and experienced. Ellen, Sara, and Becky teased me because on the bus I would sit close to Eli, our tour guide, bombarding him with questions. "Stop!" they told me. "You keep asking him questions – one after another. Give the guy a break."

But I was curious about everything.

On our tour of a kibbutz, I mentioned research I'd read about how children reared there were more skilled in groups but had more difficulty with one-on-one relationships than children raised in a nuclear family. "Dad," Sara said. "You knew that?"

It was the first evidence I'd had since her childhood, that Sara believed I actually had important information – and impressively, it was something that related to Judaism and the kibbutz.

I have other memories of trips with Sara. She attended Oberlin College in Ohio, and I drove her there in a car my parents had bought for her. It was good father/daughter time – something we'd rarely had.

Sara graduated from Oberlin College in the late nineties with three majors: Neuroscience, Judaic and Near Eastern Studies, and Biology. I felt so proud of her, even a downpour couldn't dampen my pleasure.

There is nothing like traveling, especially to places with different cultures. It shakes us out of our own often narrow views and broadens our horizons. There are so many different ways to live.

Ellen, Becky, and I visited Sara in Zimbabwe where she was doing a semester of her junior year, and we visited each of the three places she stayed. We went on a safari, which I found unbelievably exciting. I've always loved being in the back country searching for wildlife, and communing with nature. And here I was, in an open jeep-type vehicle, fully immersed in looking for lions, leopards, eagles, and all the exotic animals that inhabit parts of Africa. Watching the sun set over a watering hole while drinking a glass of wine with my family in the bush was a kind of heaven.

Becky was eighteen on that trip and wanted to bungee jump off a high bridge over the Zambezi River. I wanted to say no, but didn't think I had that right. Still, I was terrified, right down in the core of me.

She jumped.

My heart plummeted with her. And although She was fine, I'm sure she took a year or two of my life with her.

Figure 11 Becky bungee jumping over Zambezi River in Zimbabwe 1998

After returning to America and graduating from college, Sara was accepted into the prestigious Pre-IRTA program that saw her doing AIDS research at the National Institute of Health in Washington D.C. for two years in the infectious diseases division, conducting her research under Dr. Anthony Faucci.

Then she started medical school and my pride in her took another leap forward. Five years later, I had the meaningful experience of "hooding" her at her medical school graduation.

During that time between college and medical school, Sara and I went to Alaska. She'd heard me talk about a lifelong desire to visit our northernmost state to experience real wilderness, and one day, she simply said, "Let's go!" Like me, she also loved the outdoors, and I think we both wanted to share a special experience.

We flew to Anchorage, spent the night in a B&B, and flew out the next morning to Port Alsworth, a tiny community 165 miles north of Anchorage and the only one within the vast wilderness of Lake Clark National Park and Preserve. Our single engine plane carried us below the mountaintops over an endless expanse of wilderness punctuated by glacial rivers, and not a single sign of civilization as far as we could see.

From there, we embarked on a week-long rafting trip down the Chilikadrotna River: Sara, our guide, a national park historian, and me. Our guide was about thirty-five and the historian about fifty-five. At fifty-eight, I was the oldest and in pretty good shape, but when we stopped to hike on most days, the others could almost run up the mountains compared to my more measured pace.

The trip was both exhilarating and petrifying, the line between the two blurring constantly. Just understanding how far away we were from help if we ever needed it, was enough to rouse in me equal parts elation and panic.

One day, I was steering the raft, fighting to control it. And there up ahead – something in the river. I peered at it: a grizzly sow and two cubs swimming to the opposite shore. The distance between us was possibly twenty feet and closing fast. The guide jumped into my seat, taking control, trying to steer away from the bear.

The grizzly turned her enormous head, and took powerful strokes toward us. Just when we were convinced she was going to attack, she turned and swam for the shore. Passing her, we saw her heave herself up on the shore, her cubs beside her.

I don't know how long it took for my heartbeat to return to anywhere near normal.

The entire adventure was a once-in-a-lifetime experience, but the emotions Sara and I felt and shared during that week, made it even more memorable. We both remember the mosquitoes, although Sara bore the brunt of their vicious bites, even through protective clothing. One night, near the end of the trip, after a day of chilly rain, we were in our tent, camped on a sandbar, when I said, "You know, honey, coming to Alaska has always been one of my goals. But if I ever want to come back here, please remind me how f***ing hard this is."

To this day, she likes to tease me about that. And yes, it was tough, but it was also exhilarating and wonderful to be sharing it all with Sara.

In retrospect, the Alaska trip made me confront my vulnerability in ways I'd not done before. I was hours or days away from help, couldn't keep up with the others on hikes, and had little if any control over what we did and how we did it.

Figure 12 Sara and me Lake Clark National Park, Alaska, 2001

Becky didn't shy away from adventures either. In 1999, she enrolled in Semester at Sea, a program that takes college students on a three-month trip around the world, with their studies based on their destinations. I was proud of her for taking such a courageous step. With no internet, she would essentially be on her own. Ellen and I flew to Vancouver to wave her off. I stood on the dock at Coal Harbor as the ship cast off, walking down toward the end of the pier as it passed under the Lion's Gate Bridge, still waving, tears clouding my vision. Was my little girl going to be okay? She was not only okay, but grew in her perspective and confidence.

She completed the second semester of her junior year at The University of South Wales, in Sydney, Australia. She then did her senior year in Washington, D.C., graduating from George Washington University with a major in psychology. Again, I was bursting with pride. She was clearly developing into a thoughtful, interesting, confident, tolerant, clear thinking young adult.

After Becky graduated, she lived at home about five months and then moved to Australia for a short work stint. Upon returning, she moved to Boston where she worked with Habitat for Humanity through Americorps. I had a special experience driving out to Boston with her to help her get settled. Five years later, Ellen and I were thrilled to welcome her back to Denver and have her near us again.

A couple of years after moving back, Becky had an epiphany that touched us deeply. She was on a clear success track with a for-profit company when she decided it wasn't meshing with her values. She called us in tears one night saying she was going to quit her job and burgeoning career to go back to school to get an MSW. With that under her belt, she worked for several non-profits. When Ellen and I learned about the good work these organizations did, we volunteered some of our time, a decision that was meaningful to all of us.

In 2003, Sara met Gregg and introduced him to us. He had his doctorate in psychology, and although he had specialized in child psychology, he quickly became fascinated with the work I was doing.

I think he put me on a pedestal. He admired me, liked me, trusted me, and gave me more attention than I'd ever had as an adult. Saying that I felt good in his company doesn't begin to describe it.

He got me. And I got him too.

He asked questions, not because it was the right thing to do, but because he was genuinely curious and deeply interested in what I had to say. The more we talked, the more we discovered our shared ideas, thoughts, and values.

As our relationship grew and we spent more time in each other's company, we agreed that if we could wave a magic wand, we'd buy a ranch on a huge acreage nestled in a remote valley, surrounded by snow-capped peaks, with wildlife all around us.

Gregg was like the son I never had. Quite simply, I loved him to the depths I'm capable of loving, certainly almost as much as I loved my daughters.

Not long after meeting Gregg, Sara took an eighteen-month sabbatical from med school to work in Kenya doing research work on AIDS. Ellen and I had already formed a strong independent relationship with Greg. He wasn't just our daughter's boyfriend he was already part of our family. My dad had recently died, and many nights while Sara was away, he would pick up my mom and bring her to our house for dinner.

Gregg and I began working together and consulted with a company in New Jersey for a year or more. I wanted to teach him everything I knew. Working with him was gratifying and exciting. We talked non-stop about the work, our clients, the dynamics of the business, and the issues and possible solutions. We were as enthusiastic and keyed-up as I'd been after my first consulting session with Smith & Company – unable to sleep because so much was running through my mind.

In 2005, after she'd been away for about a year, Ellen and I visited Sara in Kenya. Again, my emotions were thoroughly jumbled. One of the most frightening aspects was her living arrangement. Instead of staying in an expat community, she was renting an apartment in the core of Nairobi, in a small complex with a locked gate and security guard. Her apartment had iron doors and iron bars on the windows. At the foot of the stairs to her bedroom was a "rape gate" designed to prevent anyone who managed to break past all other safeguards from getting to her upstairs room.

Seeing my daughter living alone in a place where protections like that were necessary was unsettling in the extreme.

We also visited the guarded public hospital where she was conducting her research. Armed soldiers were ubiquitous in the city. During our time there, Sara borrowed a car that we used to tour western Kenya for a week. The owner of a nearby hotel told us afterwards he'd never heard of white people going off like that on our own.

I soon understood why.

We drove on narrow, tooth-rattling, potholed roads often with semis towing two trailers in front of us, behind us, and passing us with no regard for safety or rules of the road, if indeed there were any. Many times, we were sure we were about to die in a fiery crash.

We would pull into a town or a gas station for fuel and instantly be surrounded by a troop of young men. Oddly, the experience was like being in Israel – but, at the same time, the polar opposite. In Israel, I'd felt relaxed in a way I hadn't previously experienced because I was surrounded by other Jews, and for the first time, I didn't have to think or worry about people making antisemitic comments. I was no longer part of a minority group.

In Kenya, we were a singular minority. I had never thought of myself as a racist, but suddenly I became aware of the inbred assumptions and stereotypes I'd grown up with. They were so much a part of me, I wasn't aware they existed. But there they were, lurking in dark, hidden corners of my mind. Like so many white people, I had a fear of young black males. Why? Where did that come from? Society? Media? Generational indoctrination? Possibly all of those and more. In Kenya, I was afraid of young, black men. It was a sensation not unlike how I'd felt walking back to my car after Martin Luther King was murdered and I was afraid that the two guys walking toward me would assault me. In Kenya, I was, a sixty-two-year-old white man traveling with two white women.

My eyes were opened. How must it feel to be a black man in Mississippi or Alabama or New York or Ohio? Perhaps for the first time, I had a glimmer of understanding, but it was still a tainted perception. No matter what situation I found myself in, I was still white and with that came unspoken privilege. African Americans do not come from that place of privilege – not ever – not even if they happen to be a doctor, a lawyer, or the President of the United States. The ingrained privilege of the white person, particularly the white male person, has a history that goes back too far.

Now, when I am in a setting with white people where one or two black people are present, I have an awareness I never felt before. What is it like for them? Still today – even in our supposed enlightened and progressive society – what is that like? To a small degree, I have an inkling how it feels.

Thanks to my kids, directly and indirectly, I've learned a lot. When Becky got her Master's in Social Work, she invited us to participate in some workshops on the subject of privilege. I'd had no idea about it, but my eyes were opened wide. So many concepts operate below our consciousness in society. We never pause to consider notions like privilege and how they affect every aspect of our lives.

CHAPTER 21

HONORING MY PARENTS

When I left Smith and Company in 1996, I'd started spending more time with my dad. He was getting older and starting to decline. We talked almost every night, mostly about my work. He was deeply interested in what I was doing – and I believe he was proud of me. I think we both enjoyed the close connection we were forging, and I think dad was also determined that I should have a closer relationship with my mother. He ended each phone call with, "Do you want to say hi to your mother?"

Of course I did, and asked about her activities and volunteer work. My mother and I had a strong intellectual connection, but it wasn't quite the same as what I had with my dad.

In 1999, he celebrated his ninetieth birthday by taking the entire family, including Ellen and our daughters and Mary and her two girls to a dude ranch in Colorado for a week. My mother and father had both ridden horses most of their lives. My dad was especially comfortable around them and loved riding.

I still have an image of my mother and dad at the dude ranch, dad riding beautifully – and mom wasn't a slouch in the saddle either. We had terrific days there, the mountains shining in the sun, horses moving effortlessly beneath us, and evenings with sing-alongs and campfires. I even had my first zipline experience, exhilarating once I realized it was safe.

On our last night, the ranch staff gave a gift to the most deserving person that week. Not surprisingly, of the thirty or forty-some guests there, they singled out my dad, handing him a box emblazoned with cowboy boots.

Wow! What a fabulous gift!

Dad stood up, opened the box, and threw his head back, roaring with laughter.

No – not cowboy boots - the box was full of horse manure.

Figure 13 Dad opening surprise gift on his 90th birthday

That image is etched even more firmly in my mind than the picture of him sitting tall and proud in the saddle.

A few months after that, he came home one day after picking up the laundry and fell. He didn't break anything, but it was a tangible reminder that he was getting old. He declined gradually in the next five years, and it was unimaginably hard for me to watch him lose his vigor and sharpness.

I visited almost every day. My mother and dad both needed more help, and I was happy to do it. But it was also becoming clear to me that I didn't have a lot of time left with them. More than once, they would say, "You don't need to do this. You have your own life."

Dad was especially adamant. Even years earlier when I'd told him I was thinking about moving back home from Vancouver, he'd discouraged me, pointing out that I had a great job and we were doing well, building our own lives.

Now that my parents were older and needed help, I was as adamant as my dad. "Look," I would say. "I want to do this. You gave so much to me. It's my turn to give back. It's meaningful to me. I'm not just doing it for you – I'm getting something out of it as well."

I was fortunate I had time to build beautiful memories with dad during those years before he died. He started using a walker, and one day we were making our way around the block when a beautiful twenty-something blond rode by us on her bicycle. We looked at her – the same thought bubble appearing over our heads: "She's very attractive!"

And suddenly dad picked up as much speed as he was capable off, holding onto his walker and chasing down the street after her with feeble steps. I don't know what he would have done with her if he'd caught her, but the incident can still make me smile.

The last couple of years, dad drifted in and out of dementia. There were times his mind was clear and full of insights; other times his mind seemed to float away. But we found great caregivers. Dad was never shy about speaking up if things weren't exactly the way he thought they ought to be, and one time he told the caregiver he was angry because the hotel had not delivered the food he'd ordered and he wanted to call down to the front desk to ask what had happened to his order – and why was it so late? He didn't want to eat cold food.

The caregiver, a super young man named Mike, picked up the phone, pretended to dial, and said, "Front desk please!" A pause. "Where's the food? We don't want it to get cold. Please send it up."

Dad settled back in his chair, satisfied that the issue had been handled correctly.

In spite of any hurts or disappointments I'd felt as a child, I wanted to let my parents know how much I loved and appreciated them. I wrote an essay for each of them, thinking this would be something that might be read at their funeral service. But then I realized I wanted to show this to them. I wanted them to know how I felt while they were still alive. Why do we wait until people die to express all the nice things we want to say about them? I went back over the papers, changing the tense from past to present, and handed the essays over to them.

I am so glad I did. I hope they were glad too. My dad said, "Andy, this is so much BS."

"No dad," I said. "I really mean it."

This is what I wrote and gave to my dad:

"It is impossible to sum up 92 fully lived years in a way that captures all the aspects and nuances that are unique to any individual. People are very complex and relationships are replete with many dynamics, shifts, and phases, as time marches on. Your years were filled with living and teaching values and goals that have defined your essence and helped shape my ideas of what is important in life. I identify additional examples or ideas about how you have influenced me and what you stand for each time I re-look at this document. However, it's developed to the point that I want to share it with you.

"You have several very important values that are integrated into everything you do and talk about. You believe in "taking the sweet with the sour," protecting, caring for, and teaching your family, living humbly and enduring some hardship, persistence, constantly challenging yourself and others for their best, hard work, being independent and making up your mind, and of course, always getting the very best "deal" you can. These values and perspectives are indelibly ingrained in my mind and shape much of my behavior and I have tried to impart them to my children.

"'Dadun,' as I called you when I was a little boy, has congratulated me on accomplishments but almost always you combine the congratulations with a reminder that I have to 'remember the good times to help when times are not so good.' You are always quick to remind me that life has its ups and downs and it is best lived by not "getting too excited about the ups or too upset about the downs." I have always tried to find accomplishments I could tell you about in hopes you would express your pride in me and tell me you thought I'd done a good job. Your explicit communications of love have been rare but I have never doubted your love or support. I don't think you have wanted to risk the possibility that I would become complacent or cocky or that I would over-do the excitement and risk being down or discouraged when things inevitably went sour- which you often reminded me they would. Your approach would frustrate me but you taught me to have thick skin, at least as much as an emotional person like me can have. Your approach consistently comes to my mind when I am excited about something and I remind myself that I should savor the moment because I have to try and prepare myself for disappointments, too. You have always looked ahead toward the next challenge and never gloated or spent much time rejoicing over your own achievements. You told me 'I don't stop to count how well I am doing; I just keep trying to do better.' You exemplified these values recently by sharing your thoughts about handling your increasing physical and mental challenges in a dignified way. 'I do the best I can' and have to "accept things as they come" are examples of your words of wisdom you shared to rationalize to yourself and to continue to teach me about accepting life's challenges. You have uncommon "common sense" and perspective about life that few have and you constantly drive home your thinking. I find myself repeating many of your words and ideas in my own mind and to others as well.

"Protecting and caring for your family, even great grandchildren yet to be born, has always been a driving force for you. You see your role in the old fashioned way- it's the man's responsibility and duty to take care of his family and to see to it that his offspring are given the tools to live successfully and endure hardships. You are very proud of your family but always with perspective. You talk about the strengths and weaknesses of your grandparents, uncles, and cousins. The importance of family extends to mother's family too. You have consistently encouraged me to learn about that side of my heritage and on almost every phone call you see to it that I talk with mom as well as you. Your sense of family loyalty is very strong. All of us regularly receive reading material on topics relevant to our interests or on items you believe we should be more aware of. You saw your role and felt responsibility to be a surrogate father for Aimee and Sunny when Bob became sparse in their lives. You spend individual time with each grandchild. For years you have taken them out to lunch and have commented how special it is to get to know each one alone. It has enabled you to really relate to each of them in a special, individualized, and significant fashion. You often mention how special each grandchild is in her own way; how each has her their own strengths and it is their strengths you emphasize. You express concern occasionally about how a grandchild is handling some aspect of themselves or their lives and expect yourself to be able to help each granddaughter overcome whatever obstacle you are worried they are confronting. You have advised me that nothing is more important than family and during a recent family crisis situation reminded me that I belonged with Ellen and Becky, not at work.

"You believe that material self-indulgence is to be avoided and that learning to live with what you have, not what you want, is a virtue. You, like mom, share the philosophy that living well within ones means is very important. I remember going with you many years ago and talking with a man who wanted to buy an apartment you built and developed. The person told you that selling the business would enable you to buy a new car and that you did not have to drive the 'old Ford convertible' you came to the meeting in. When we were back in the car after the meeting you told me you were perfectly happy with your old car and had no need or desire to buy a new one. I think you were insulted that the man thought a new car would entice you to sell the apartment to him. External, material signs of success mean very little to you. You were not only satisfied sitting in an old beat up desk chair for years and years but you resisted buying one to help your back until you decided to buy a chair for me too. The chair we eventually bought was used and stained but 'it would work just fine.' You pride yourself on using what you have, not on what you could have. The satisfaction of 'building something' and shunning symbols of success are part of your character.

"Your high standards are evident in your very early art work where you drew carefully, symmetrically, and clearly. You are a perfectionist and drive yourself and all of us to measure up to your standards, even sometimes to your way of doing something. I can't remember you raising your voice or losing your temper but I am never in doubt about what you think or what you hope I will do in any given situation. You expected anybody who did work with or for you to perform to your level. Sometimes we did and sometimes we didn't. I remember many hours of helping you fix things in our house or in property you owned. Taking the easier road to repair something would satisfy me but you always pushed me, and yourself, to 'do it right.' You often reminded me that 'anything worth doing was worth doing right.' When we failed to live up to your expectations there was always a reminder and prodding to 'look into it some more' or 'let's do it this way.' You challenge yourself constantly. You are very proud of volunteering to serve in the Marine Corps. If you had to fight you wanted the best training possible and you wanted to be a part of the elite you admired since childhood. You entered the Marine Corps at the age of 34 and although you were often last in the physical training regimens, because of competing with men much younger, you are extremely proud that you endured and successfully conquered the challenges. You have been especially proud that you did nothing to avoid serving overseas, unlike many others in your outfit. You 'took things as they came' and believed you would find a way to cope no matter what developed. You are a man of courage. You attribute your Marine Corps experience to many of your post service values and behaviors although I think these values were a part of your character long before the Marine Corps. You climbed stairs two at a time in rapid fashion until you were around ninety years old. Challenging yourself is not only accomplished physically. You studied business and other issues that interested you in great detail and thoroughness. For example, your financial advisor said you are the only client he has had who really read companies' annual reports and analyzed them to inform your investing decisions. You taught me the importance of asking others their thinking as a way to bring them out and understand and enlarge my own thinking.

"Being independent and making something of yourself by yourself is another value and goal you strive to accomplish and have been able to achieve; although your own standards probably leave you thinking you still have a long way to go to live up to your expectations of yourself. You have worked very hard. You spent countless hours at your basement desk and other places 'doing chores.' Often day and night you were working to better yourself, reach your goals, and prove you could become financially successful largely on your own, and provide security for your family. Still, in spite of your very strong work ethic, you probably never missed a little league game of mine and encouraged me on during many practices as well. I think you were the only parent to win a letter because of your constant and enthusiastic support of the Bombers. You talked about how your grandfather provided security for his family and you tried to model yourself in a similar manner. Your independence and strong personality sometimes led to difficulties with those with whom you came into contact but I believe most still respected you and your dedication to 'do things the right way' and to measure up to your high standards. You taught me to stand up for myself, to not take no for an answer when I was chasing something important, but always to be assertive in a respectful manner. You understood the importance of 'who you know' on getting things accomplished and drove this point home to me in a compelling and indelible way. Sometimes you do not mince words with others and it embarrasses me, but I always understand the point you are trying to make and the goal you are trying to achieve. You emphasize doing as much for yourself as you can. Recently, it has frustrated me when you would not let me help you out of a car, but you insisted on doing it by yourself; you do not want to give in to anything until there is no choice.

"The community and giving back to it were always important to you. You began your long and distinguished volunteer career working at the Auraria Community Center. You eventually served many terms on their Board of Directors and were the only non-Hispanic who was not pushed to resign from the Board during the turbulent 60's. That made me feel very proud of you. You also were critical in helping to plan and build a new community center building. Your other community passion, among several, was birth control. You served on the Colorado Planned Parenthood Board and strongly believed that population control is the basic salvation of our planet. You raised us to always "clean up after ourselves" and we learned very early that littering was wrong. Your example helped set the course for my professional pursuits, although you never pushed me in any way toward what to pursue in my work life. You have always encouraged me to do my best, apply myself, and the results would speak for themselves.

"The gratitude I feel toward you and the indelible values and attitudes you tried to model and always encouraged will shine brightly, forever, in my mind. You should feel very proud of the impact you have had on your family and community. Your core values of taking the good with the bad, taking care of your family, living humbly and enduring some hardship, persistence, setting high standards and being independent, and contributing to the community are clear. I only hope I can provide some of the same inspiration to my kids that you provide to me. As you taught me, I will do my best and not give up. 'Everything in the world every time you can think of it.'"

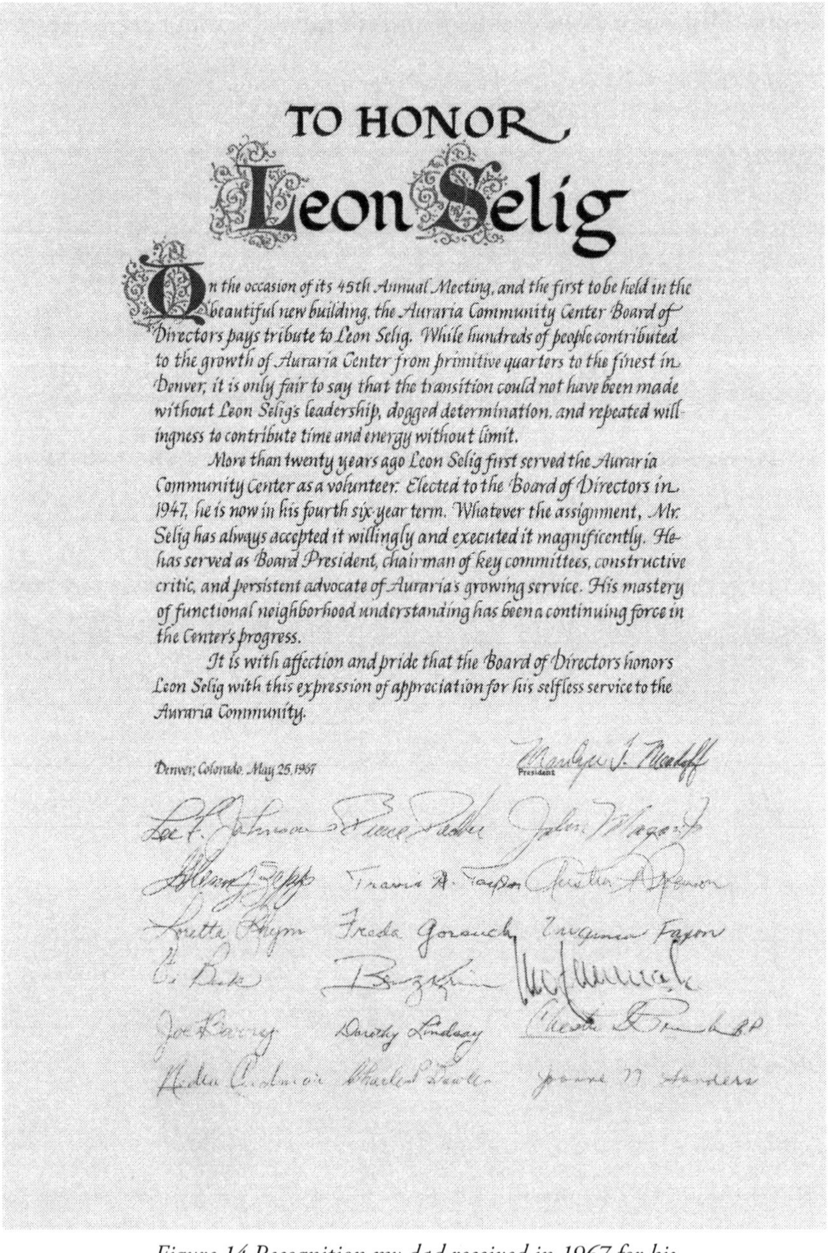

TO HONOR

Leon Selig

On the occasion of its 45th Annual Meeting, and the first to be held in the beautiful new building, the Auraria Community Center Board of Directors pays tribute to Leon Selig. While hundreds of people contributed to the growth of Auraria Center from primitive quarters to the finest in Denver, it is only fair to say that the transition could not have been made without Leon Selig's leadership, dogged determination, and repeated willingness to contribute time and energy without limit.

More than twenty years ago Leon Selig first served the Auraria Community Center as a volunteer. Elected to the Board of Directors in 1947, he is now in his fourth six-year term. Whatever the assignment, Mr. Selig has always accepted it willingly and executed it magnificently. He has served as Board President, chairman of key committees, constructive critic, and persistent advocate of Auraria's growing service. His mastery of functional neighborhood understanding has been a continuing force in the Center's progress.

It is with affection and pride that the Board of Directors honors Leon Selig with this expression of appreciation for his selfless service to the Auraria Community.

Denver, Colorado, May 25, 1967

President

Figure 14 Recognition my dad received in 1967 for his decades of service at a community center in Denver

For my mother, I wrote the following:

"January, 2005

"To My Mommy,

"I have been working on this for months, and while it will never be "finished" it's close enough to share with you.

" Abraham Lincoln is still alive as far as I am concerned. I thought of you that way as a little boy and the image has not changed. It signifies to me your deep motivation to understand others in need and your sometimes-tireless efforts to help them surmount their problems. Over many years you volunteered with or helped start many organizations, the ones I remember being The Santa Claus Shop, Planned Parenthood, Temple Micah, Human Services, Inc., The Children's Hospital Blood Bank, Newborn Center, and Family Care Center. The Child Welfare League of America honored you as an Outstanding Board Member. You have not been primarily interested in building buildings, setting strategy, planning or running events or fund raising, although you probably helped in all these areas. I do remember your experience lobbying the State Legislature many years ago and the extreme reactions some Catholic priests demonstrated in response to the lobbying efforts. Your main calling has been to help others in a direct, literally "hands on manner." You wrote letters to families to tell them about their baby when they lived far away from the hospital. You seem to have a special empathy for loneliness in others. You seem to sense when others feel especially alone and you extend yourself to them, especially those who are helpless like infants and young children.

"You have rocked, fed, and soothed literally hundreds of infants. You are totally "there" for people in need and you have an intuitive sense of what people need and how to make them feel better. Your recent response to my surgery is the latest example. Your presence was soothing, your words encouraging and wise, your food filled a void, and your concern and empathy helped me tolerate and get through a very hard time. You were one of the first people selected to receive the very special 9 Who Care Award in 1982. Receiving the 9 Who Care Award was a momentous occasion and one that you felt somewhat uncomfortable with. Public recognition has never been your motive nor have you been comfortable with it, although you have received it on numerous occasions.

"At the grass-roots level, you have given to so many babies and their families over the years that it's almost not a surprise anymore when you run into somebody who remembers you and what you did for them. Just last year on our way to Boston, an airline ticket agent recognized you and remembered how much you had helped her many years before. We have been in restaurants eating dinner when people have come to the table and introduced themselves to you, once again recalling how you extended yourself to them at some meaningful point in their past.

"Your belief that nobody should die alone is indelibly etched into my head; I only hope I can fulfill that belief for my loved ones. You have soothed dying babies and held them in your hands when they died. You can "be there" for somebody else to a level that and at times when many others are trying to avoid the situation. This belief and the behavior to support it, is another inspiring trait of yours that sets the bar high for me.

"You are tolerant and give others the benefit of the doubt but are very loyal to your family. Almost any time somebody has disappointed you, your first response is to speculate on their motivation and to express understanding for their behavior. You try to empathize and view their behavior from the standpoint of an optimistic and positive perspective. You can be very different if you perceive somebody to have wronged somebody you love; your responses in these situations are fiercely loyal and you defend your loved one. Your empathy for "the underdog" is always evident. You defend those you love with zeal, even to the point of sometimes overlooking their own shortcomings.

"You are the consummate 'lady' even though you haven't necessarily liked the image. You are poised, graceful and calm, yet you can softly express your opinions and thoughts. You shun aggressiveness and prefer tolerance and acceptance, but you quietly and independently pursue what you want to do. I will never forget your going back to Rose Hospital parking lot and throwing an egg at the car after its driver had rudely pulled in front of you to take a parking place you were waiting for. The 'egg incident' didn't make you less a lady to me, but it was an example of your sense of humor, your willingness to push the boundaries of convention every once in a while, and your ability to stand up for yourself when you deemed it important enough to do so.

"You take pride in your appearance and always dress in a non-ostentatious but classy manner. You have a sense of humor that some people may miss because they think of you as contained and proper. While you can be contained and proper, you also like to laugh and have fun. You took dad's teasing, and some of mine, for years. You would often have a quick comeback even when it initially appeared you were ignoring what was said. You also like to laugh at a good joke and can do a good job of telling some yourself.

"I attribute a substantial part of whatever intellectual proclivities and curiosities I have to you. You always read a great deal and talked about some of the values and ideas you derived from your reading. You sensitized me to how an author can sculpt somebody's personality to a level that makes it feel like you really know the person. You studied current events for years and it helped stimulate my curiosity about the world around me. Introducing me to The Conference on World Affairs and going to meetings together and discussing the ideas we heard was a significant turning point for me. It made me aware of so many 'things' in the world, from Buckmaster Fuller and geodesic domes to the United Nations, to China, to the impact of the media, and so on. I think a lot of my intellectual curiosity, such as it is, can be traced back to these exposures. You never pushed this on me because that's really never been your approach. You modeled 'being aware' and encouraged it when you saw it in me. This has enriched my life tremendously and I hope I have been able to pass some of it on to my kids.

"You helped me realize the importance and benefits of knowing about my heritage. Your pride in your background has helped pique my interest in knowing more about the values, personalities, and experiences of my family members that came before I did. This sense of heritage, history, and accomplishment helps give me roots, pride, and a sense of what I hope, in some small way, I can live up to.

"You exemplify 'love begetting love' and have modeled this as far back as I can remember. I remember very clearly how attentive you were to your parents, how you respected them, gave to them, and helped teach me the critical value of being respectful to others. You have lovingly knitted many pieces of clothing, many of them showing evidence of your creativity, as well as your knitting prowess, for all of us for many years. Hopefully, you're really neat baby blankets will soothe generations of family babies in the future. While you are not disrespectful of material things, you emphasize relationships and enjoying life. You don't let yourself get distracted by the 'cracks in the driveway' and you encourage me to think about this perspective, as well.

"Your acceptance helped balance Dad's continual emphasis on improvement. I'm not implying you haven't valued becoming a better person, or that you haven't encouraged me do be and do better, but you have balanced that emphasis with a tolerance for difference and an open-mindedness that means a great deal to me. Your wisdom has been helpful to me and will stick with me forever. The biggest example, I think, is your telling me many years ago that we never 'get over' certain people and that it's futile and unrealistic to expect anything different. This advice helped me get beyond a big hurdle. I have shared the same idea with many people, and it's had a similar, substantial impact on them, too.

"Another impressive characteristic you have is the ability to develop and maintain friendships with people who are much younger. Your interest in them, the model you set for giving to others, and your awareness of 'what's going on in the world' probably combine to draw younger people to you. The most recent example was when several couples brought dinner over to your house, prepared it, served it, and cleaned it all up before they left. I think some must see you as a surrogate mother because of your interest in them and your compassion for them in times of difficulty.

"You have courage and face life's challenges with acceptance. Your attitude about leaving the house you (and all of us) love and moving to Park Place is the most recent example. You accept life's facts: we can't change certain things and therefore have to willingly and maturely make changes that are not necessarily ones we want to make. You suffered with severe migraine headaches for most all of your adult life. I remember many times when I was growing up, that you would quietly lie down in bed with ice on your head. You never complained and you never used your headaches as an excuse to avoid responsibility. You minimize your hurts and pain, sometimes to the point that I have gotten upset because I wanted to give back to you some of what you have given to me, and because I've wanted to do everything possible to be helpful to you.

"So, your impact has been deep and broad, and forever appreciated. Mostly, I think, I admire your ability to give to others and your effort to live by the Golden Rule. It's a high standard to set and one I strive to do better at. I still sincerely mean I love you as much as 'Everything in the world every time you can think of it.'"

Figure 15 My mother in Children's Hospital Newborn Center holding a sick baby and announcement of her being selected for special recognition by a local television station.

My dad died just before his ninety-fifth birthday on April 4, 2004. He was in home hospice for the last six months of his life – days and weeks I found intensely difficult. During that time he contracted a C. difficile infection treated by a powerful antibiotic that not only attacked the C. difficile in his colon, but also his body's beneficial bacteria. During the treatment, he got a tooth infection and was too infirm to visit a dentist, so we brought one to the house to extract the tooth.

Shortly after the extraction, his mouth became infected, which, we believe, became a systemic infection. Though his passing became imminent then, I still had no doubt in my mind that my dad wanted to live. He'd talked about fighting to survive and I was determined to give him every tool possible in that battle.

And I didn't want to let him go.

Toward the end, when he was clearly dehydrated, I wanted hospice to give him fluids. My sister and mom disagreed. They believed we should let him go. I prevailed, but it was too late.

We were all with him when he died, and as his spirit passed, my mom said, "Smell him. You'll never get that smell again."

He had a particular unique smell that I recalled from childhood, and smell is closely linked to memory.

Then she removed his Marine Corps ring and gave it to me. I've never worn it – just kept it safe.

After that, Sara and I stood inside my parent's front door as the mortuary carried my dad away. Together, we yelled, "Baaaa," which has been a tradition in my family when we parted from one another.

A couple of weeks after my dad died, I experienced some intermittent intestinal symptoms for about twenty-four hours, and at about 10 p.m., I felt excruciating abdominal pains. I went to the hospital with Ellen, and sat in the emergency room while the world began to disappear. Was I dying?

My body slumped lower in the chair. Everything went away. I know I had an X-ray, but the details escape me. They diagnosed appendicitis, but when the surgeon opened me up, he found a ruptured appendix. Thankfully he got to it in time and cleaned it up.

After a couple of nights in the hospital, and after being back home a couple of days, I told Ellen I was going for a walk.

"Okay," she said. "But take it easy. Don't go too far."

I walked three miles and ended up back in the hospital, in acute pain at the surgery site. The surgeon debated whether he should go back in to clean up the infection. In the end and to my relief, he decided not to.

It was a hard lesson for me to learn – I wasn't superman, and pushing through was not always the best route. For the next couple of months, I put my feet up, forcing myself to be idle. When I declared myself recovered, I drove up into the mountains, laced up my hiking boots, and strode out on the trail. It felt so good to move my body and to feel it responding with health and strength.

My mom stayed in the house for about a year after my father died before moving into an independent living facility. I continued to talk to her every day and visited often. Her health was good but she had a bad hip – bone on bone. Her doctor had told her a few years previously that she was eligible for a hip replacement. She declined, but over the years the pain got so bad she had to stop volunteering and driving.

Eventually, pain killers were not enough to dull her hip pain. Starting morphine helped, but the longer-term effects on her GI system were intolerable. And then she started to fail and we asked hospice to come. Soon after that, Sara and Gregg flew out from Boston. Their visit seemed to lift her spirits.

She'd always said she wasn't afraid of death, and it was clear that she made the decision to die when she judged the quality of her life untenable. Rather than experience any further deterioration or get caught up in the arguments Mary and I were having, she removed her oxygen mask and stopped eating and drinking. A few days later, on May 9, 2008, she died.

Even now, few days go by that I don't think about my parents.

CHAPTER 22

GREGG

In 2004, not long after Sara arrived in Kenya, she threw out her back and Gregg flew over to be with her. After that, he would spend several weeks at a time working in Denver and then several weeks in Kenya with Sara. After about a year, with Sara's help, he received a grant from the Clinton Foundation to deliver training to Kenyan child development workers.

In Kenya, Gregg and Sara worked in close proximity but independently. He loved the country as much as Sara did. They liked the culture, the art, and the people, and hoped to marry and continue working in both Kenya and the United States. Meanwhile, Sara returned from Kenya in the spring of 2006 to resume medical school. Gregg joined her shortly afterwards.

On October 31, 2006, Gregg was jogging when he noticed that he had visual disturbances in his left eye. What was going on? He couldn't shake it and visited an ophthalmologist who sent him to a retina specialist who diagnosed ocular melanoma.

The disease is extraordinarily rare, affecting only about two thousand people per year in America – and it is fatal in fifty percent of cases.

Devastating.

I remember getting the call and meeting Sara and Gregg with Ellen in the foyer of the doctor's office building where he had just been given his diagnosis. His next stop was the Wills Eye Center at the Thomas Jefferson Medical School in Philadelphia, one of the few places in the country with expertise in ocular melanoma. They radiated his primary tumor.

Ellen and I flew to Philadelphia to be by his and Sara's side, but weren't allowed to get close to him due to the radioactive material used.

We desperately hoped Gregg would be one of the fifty percent whose cancer didn't spread to other parts of his body, and we lived the next days and months in dread and hope. Surely, nothing bad could happen to this wonderful man.

In the spring of 2007, while Sara was away learning medical Spanish, Gregg asked Ellen and me out to dinner. We suspected a purpose behind the invitation. We were nervous with anticipation through drinks and dinner, and even into dessert. He said nothing of personal import. One glance at Ellen told me she felt as let down as I was. Then, when we'd given up all hope, he asked the "question." Would we support his proposal of marriage to Sara? We couldn't say yes fast enough. Sometime later, he invited Sara on a trip to the mountains in Marble, Colorado, where he proposed to her on horseback. Obviously, we were thrilled.

Figure 16 Ellen, Sara, Becky, Myself, and Gregg. Jackson Hole, Wyoming, 2007

For the next several months, Gregg and Sara continued to live in Denver, where Sara was attending medical school. She graduated in May 2007, and soon after that, they moved to Boston so Sara could start her residency in Internal Medicine and Global Health Equity. On November 7 of that year, Gregg flew back to Philadelphia for the checkup he had every couple of months. While he was in the waiting room before his appointment, he called, leaving a message on our machine, to ask after "Grandmommie," – my mother's pet name – and to see how we were doing. An hour later the doctors gave him the news that his cancer had metastasized into his liver. In effect, it was a death sentence. He was given six months to live.

Sara completed her Global Health Equity residency program and became involved in working with Native Americans. It satisfied her passion for cross-cultural experiences, and for making a difference to people who were often deprived of the things that make for a reasonably secure life, including first class medical care.

She worked with the Navajo nation for years. Ellen and I visited the reservation more than once, and I even got involved with training community health supervisors as a volunteer. I have always been and still am excited about her work with them. After all, I was the little boy who wanted to be an Indian when we played cowboys and Indians.

Very little was known about Gregg's disease, and because of that, Gregg and Sara had a tough time finding answers – or even knowing where to begin looking. We all did as much research as possible, spending countless hours on the internet, searching worldwide for clues.

The scarcity of information and challenge of finding reliable data, led Sara to founding CURE Ocular Melanoma, an organization she now leads that supports patients and their families, helping them navigate services and information. It also convenes scientists from around the world who share their findings, ideally getting out of their silos and working together as a team. These things did not exist when Gregg was diagnosed, and there was little most patients could do after their cancer had spread.

Sara and Gregg had been planning an August 2008 wedding. Would he still be alive? The odds said no.

They decided to move up the date to January, 2008, and to change the affair to an intimate event in our living room with only a handful of guests – Gregg's best man, Sara's special friend, their spouses, Gregg's parents and brother, my mother, Becky, Ellen, and me.

We felt a certain amount of excitement, as we should when two people who love each other get married, but while I was happy for them, I was also overwhelmed with sorrow, knowing this happiness would be short-lived. My confusion of emotions – of happiness, love, and grief, was at times, disorienting.

My mother didn't come to the rehearsal dinner, which I found hurtful and hard to understand. And then, she also didn't come to our open house the day after the wedding where all our local family and all of Gregg and Sara's friends were present. What was going on?

A couple of days later, I went to my mother's apartment in the independent living complex to show her some devices that might help with her declining hearing. I tapped on the door and walked in. She wasn't there but before I could leave, I heard the telephone ring. I walked into the small kitchen to answer it and there, beside the phone, she'd left a note. It was clear she'd written it to herself, never intending to show it to anyone else. But it was impossible not to read the words on the page.

"Note to myself – Sunday 3 a.m.

"I have not slept since going to bed. The way Mary was treated, and equally how I was treated was a disgrace. The wedding may have looked beautiful, but it was mean, ugly, and very sad. It could have been beautiful had everyone's feelings been considered."

We had abided by Gregg and Sara's wishes by not inviting my sister and her children. We also didn't invite Ellen's brother or his family. Gregg's aunts, uncles and their family were also not present. In light of the situation, they felt it would have been overwhelming to have so many people at the wedding, and they didn't want to invite some and leave others out.

I called Ellen, tears choking my voice. How could my mother think I was a terrible person, when I was doing my best to fulfill my daughter and her partner's wishes? And there it was once again, just as it had been when I was a boy – the sense that she was more empathetic to Mary's feelings than mine. Okay, I could understand that Mary felt left out, but couldn't my mother see my point of view this one time? I was about to lose my son-in-law, a man I loved dearly, and my daughter was losing the love of her life. Where was her empathy for us?

The note confirmed what I'd thought all my life, that she thought of me as someone who could handle whatever came his way, while Mary needed help – specifically, her help.

That night, at about 10 or 11 p.m., still upset, I got down on the floor to do my regular push-ups, but without warming up first. Afterwards, I got into the shower where I started sweating. My throat was sore and I felt odd – weak and dizzy. Something wasn't right.

Concerned, Ellen started an internet search of my symptoms. "It could be a heart attack," she said.

There's no way I could have a heart attack! I'm in great shape. I've worked out all my life. I have no risk factors. No one in my family had a heart attack. My blood pressure is fine – really – absolutely no risk factors.

Ellen wanted to call 911 – my symptoms weren't improving.

"No," I said. "I don't want to call 911. The EMTs will come upstairs. We have a new carpet and I don't want their dirty shoes on the carpet! Let's just see how I feel in the morning."

Ellen said, "If you won't have the paramedics come, I'm going to drive you to the hospital."

She drove to the closest one, a community hospital and not a level one trauma center. On arrival, we were taken into the ER where they quickly diagnosed a heart attack.

Heart attack? Me? How can I possibly be having a heart attack?

Shock and denial couldn't change the facts.

I waited an hour before they could get me in for an angiogram, and then even longer while they called in an interventional cardiologist, who inserted two stents in the left anterior descending artery, the biggest artery in the heart, which provides fifty percent of the heart muscle's blood supply. There's a reason it's called the "widowmaker" artery.

Because of the time elapsed between entering the hospital and receiving treatment, I lost some heart function, which would not have occurred had I been less concerned about the carpet and been taken by ambulance to a major trauma center. However, my heart and health returned to normal fairly shortly. Still, Ellen and I were hyper-vigilant for the next couple of months, concerned about the slightest sensation I had in my chest. We went back to the ER a couple of times, worried about chest palpitations or odd sensations. Luckily, I was fine. The sensations were likely caused by my own fears and anxiety.

Never before had I felt so vulnerable. Just like that, in the blink of an eye, I could go from carefree robust health, to the edge of death. And I had no control over the outcome.

I took medications to lower my heart rate and started cardiac rehab, working hard to get back into shape. My therapists had to remind me to slow down. This was not a time to push myself to the extent I usually did. It wasn't too long, however, before they told me I could do anything I wanted to. My heart had returned to normal, or as close to that as possible.

CHAPTER 23

GOOD-BYE TO GREGG

Neither Sara nor Gregg nor their families ever gave up trying to find a treatment or therapy that would help Gregg manage his disease. We knew there was no cure, but there had to be something else, maybe something that would turn a terminal illness into a chronic disease.

Between treatments, Gregg and Sara did their best to live as normal a life as possible. Sometimes Gregg would get treated early in the morning and then go to work afterwards, never letting on there was anything wrong.

He saw a Chinese herbalist., He tried immunotherapy, a fairly new treatment that involved harvesting some of his cancer cells in order to get his immunological system to fight it. He saw a pulmonologist in Texas because the cancer had spread to his lungs. Although some of the treatments probably prolonged his life, none of the many avenues he walked down led to daylight.

In Texas, in the fall of 2008, we experienced a rare moment of joy when Barack Obama won the election. We were all sitting in front of the television in the hospital lobby, eating ice cream, smiles splitting our faces.

The cancer continued to spread.

In Boston, in October 2009, at the first scientific meeting Sara spearheaded, Gregg gave a powerful address. Part of his inspiring talk was aimed at convincing the scientists, who came from many different research entities, to work together as a team to understand the disease, and to find treatments to manage and eventually cure it. Gregg credited the assembled researchers for his recent success and then said:

"We now have a NEW vision – you have more than risen to the occasion to help me, my family and countless others fighting uveal melanoma – now I, we, ask that you think about yourselves just as we think about you – not divided by institution, by beliefs, by treatment expertise – but TODAY – and moving forward from today – please see yourself as a TEAM – help yourselves as a TEAM, count on one another as a TEAM, believe in each other as a TEAM, share and interact as a TEAM, break down the barriers as a TEAM, create a vision as a TEAM– please look around the room – you are so much stronger, so better off, as a TEAM.

"I represent the many others in my position - those who would like to be here today to address you - I've wondered what they might want me to say to you or what they might want to say themselves – while I'm not completely certain I think it might include: thank you so very much for assembling here and for your passionate dedication to uveal melanoma– we hope you develop some action items today that might eventually help increase understanding, research and treatments for this disease and that you move forward from today keeping our and YOUR vision alive – and that you work TOGETHER to accomplish the goals you develop here.

"We – those with this disease - are so hopeful that your collaborative work will not only advance the field but will also lengthen and hopefully save our lives.

"Thank you again so very much – you inspire us - we are so excited for what will happen here today and beyond!

"Only TOGETHER will it be possible to see and find the cure!

"Thank you."

*Figure 17 Last trip with Gregg for Ellen's 60th birthday.
Mexico. Me, Ellen, Gregg, Sara, and Becky. 2009*

In addition to the numerous places the cancer had metastasized, it also spread to his brain. There was a day he was strapped to a table while the doctors sent radiation into his skull. Gregg and Sara held hands as they walked through hell. For four years, we walked beside them as much as we could.

Twice, he had radioactive beads injected into his liver that probably did more than anything else to extend his life, so in 2011, he flew to Denver for another treatment. Sadly, the doctor said his liver was too riddled with the disease and Gregg was too ill to withstand the procedure.

That was when my hope started to drain away. They flew back to Boston where the renowned Dana-Farber/Harvard Cancer Center said they could do no more. At that point, around Thanksgiving 2011, Sara and Gregg got Hospice involved.

For about three months, between October 2011 and January 2012. Ellen and I spent most of our time in Boston, renting part of an old house some of the time, and staying in a hotel for several weeks. Our sole purpose was to help Sara and Gregg in any way we could. There were days Sara would ask us not to come by, but to please drop off some medications. I told my clients I'd be on hiatus for a while – nothing was more important to me than being there for Sara and Gregg.

Gregg began to look heartbreakingly gaunt. And I – all of us – were helpless to make it better. All we could do was our best to fill those last weeks and days with love. That was my intention when Gregg got angry with me. He'd grown up in the western part of Connecticut and wanted to go "home" one last time, and I wanted to give him the gift of that short trip. Although he asked me not to arrange a way for him to get there, I asked the local fire department to carry him from their apartment to a waiting car without consulting him. He was pretty mad that I had violated his wish, and unfortunately, he never did get back to his old home before he died.

But that was only one occasion. We had beautiful conversations before the end. His mind was as bright and clear as ever. He explained how he'd grown up in a prosperous family, where his dad, an orthodontist, earned quite a bit and didn't hesitate to spend it. I'd grown up in a family that had very little, and even when my dad started to do fairly well, we were frugal and lived beneath our means. The gist of that conversation was that perhaps I had to loosen up a bit while he could think about saving a bit more. We agreed that the sweet spot was probably somewhere in the middle where both our financial views could meet. That discussion and some others had a lasting impact on me.

Gregg died at home on January 10, 2012. We were all there: Sara, Gregg's parents, and Ellen and I. We left the room after the last breath escaped his body, leaving Sara alone with him. I'd known it was coming, and still, deep in my stomach was a pit of despair and loss.

I'd lost so much, but not as much as Sara who had to move forward in the world without her husband and best friend. How was she going to manage?

People like Gregg only come along once in a lifetime. I'd never have this person or this connection again. I hadn't just lost what we had, but what we were dreaming of for the future. All the plans we'd made – all the conversations we were going to have – all the years ahead with him and Sara and the children they might have had – all of that had vanished.

Gregg had given me something I'd longed for all my life and never had. He'd taken an interest in me. He wanted to know my opinions on everything, and he listened to my answers and asked more questions. He was genuinely attentive to me and what made me who I was. And I learned a lot from Gregg. His tolerance and acceptance of others was exceptional, as was his natural ability to ask questions as a way to move others toward something he thought was important. Gregg could certainly be assertive, but unlike the younger me, he didn't lead with it. He was also much more likely to spend money on items I'd not even consider, which tweaked my approach. More than once, Gregg said he wished his dad was more like me. Of course, I discouraged that thought. I wasn't remotely interested in undermining that relationship. But still, his words expanded my heart.

Sara organized a service for Gregg, but the best thing we did for him was "sitting shiva," the Jewish tradition where family and friends gather at the home of the deceased for seven days and mourn the loss by recollecting the loved one and telling stories.

Gregg's friends came to the apartment and talked about him, filling us with gratitude that so many people had loved him – and loved him still. We listened to stories and got a sense of the incredible impact he'd had on so many people. We all shared our sense of loss. I realized that all of us saw Gregg for the man he was: thoughtful, caring, and with a profound desire to understand the people he interacted with.

One of his friends coined the phrase, "What Would Gregg Do?" (WWGD). I still reflect on that phrase, using it as a way to cool my impulsiveness and as a reminder to step back and reflect before reacting.

One day, not long before he died, Gregg had said, "I'm just afraid that no one is going to remember me."

Those words stabbed my heart. To think that anyone could forget him! Oh the despair of believing that! He had so many people who loved him. And me? More than a dozen years after his death, I still think of him almost every day.

The one piece of the future we didn't lose was Sara and Gregg's child – our granddaughter, Giuliana. Sara and Gregg had always wanted to be parents and have their own family so they ensured that remained a possibility through Gregg's cancer journey. Although they weren't able to realize their shared dream together while Gregg was alive, they made a back-up plan. which Sara carried out after Gregg's death with his blessing. About two years after he died, Sara gave birth to Giuliana Elise Selig. Looking at Giuliana today, is like seeing a small piece of Gregg, perhaps in the shape of her smile or the sound of her laugh, or her beautiful curly hair. Of course, she is her own beautiful and strong person, and yet I see parts of both Sara and Gregg in her and I know Gregg would be beaming with pride at the young woman she is becoming. I deeply regret that he isn't there for her and her mother.

CHAPTER 24

TRAVELS

Ellen and I took some great trips over the years. I love traveling for so many reasons, but chiefly because I'm curious and I love to learn and share it all with Ellen. I also appreciate seeing new places. Traveling broadened my outlook on the world, and I did learn so much about different cultures and ways of being, thinking, and living. Probably, what I learned about most, was myself. I think traveling makes you a better person, especially if you go to places where the cultures and ways of thinking are significantly different. You discover how rich humanity is and how many ways there are to simply be.

When Becky attended a semester of her junior year in Australia in 2000, Sara, Ellen, and I visited her in Sidney. After touring her school and the city, we travelled to Cairns, known as the gateway to the northernmost section of the Great Barrier Reef. Unfortunately, we encountered rough weather and didn't see what we'd hoped to on our snorkeling trips, but we made up for it with a great comic anecdote that happily, was not at our expense.

Ellen was not feeling well, so Sara, Becky, and I boarded the boat that would take us out to the reef. About twenty or thirty Japanese tourists were our boat mates. On the trip out, the crew laid out a sumptuous brunch that the Japanese tourist group attacked with so much zeal, I could swear they hadn't eaten in days.

The seas were rough enough that I had to take a wide stance to remain upright. Perhaps it was the rolling seas or the amount of food they'd eaten or a combination of both, but before we even got to the reef, the tourists started throwing up with prolonged noisy and malodorous ferocity. The crew valiantly rushed around the deck, handing out paper bags as efficiently as they could while side-stepping digested bits of egg and shrimp on the slippery deck.

On our passage back, after a disappointing snorkel in dark, cold waters, the ship's staff bravely served another meal that the now-recovered group attacked with as much gusto as they had the earlier brunch. Trying to make up for what had been lost? This time, they managed to keep it all down.

We also visited a beautiful nature reserve, generously endowed by John Denver. I also remember talking to one of Becky's teachers who told us about the racism Australia's aboriginals had been subjected to for so many years. A visit to several museums confirmed her report. It seemed to me they were a century behind the United States in terms of dignity, respect, and human rights.

In 2013, to celebrate our fortieth anniversary and my seventieth birthday, we flew to Budapest for a river cruise on the Danube. European river cruises were practically tailor-made for us because the boat accommodated only about one hundred, and we were divided into small groups when touring specific sites. Part of our enjoyment was always meeting other people. Unfortunately, heavy rainfall in May and June created one of the largest floods in the past two centuries in the Upper Danube Basin, causing our tour company to amend the trip.

We still had a wonderful holiday, just not the one we'd expected. On our first night in the city, suffering from jetlag, we walked down to the river, where we came upon sixty pairs of shoes on the bank of the Danube not far from the Hungarian Parliament building. They were old-fashioned shoes, the type people wore in the 1940s. There were women's, men's, and children's shoes, scattered and abandoned, as though their owners had just stepped out of them and left them there. But they weren't ordinary shoes. They were rusted, made of iron and set into the concrete of the embankment as a memorial to the Hungarian Jews who, in the winter of 1944-1945, were told to step out of them before being shot by members of the Arrow Cross Party, a far-right Hungarian nationalist party closely aligned with the Nazis.

We toured the city, visiting a hot bath, an ancient synagogue, and a restaurant that served magnificent goulash, but the sculpture on the banks of the Danube remained in my mind.

Our tour company made alternate plans, sending us by bus to our riverboat destinations of Vienna and Prague. It may not have been a cruise, but we probably became even closer to our fellow travelers and we still had a terrific time. Vienna was fascinating, but it was definitely a case of too many monumental buildings and churches.

Prague, on the other hand, was a delight with friendly people in the shops and restaurants we entered. We visited the old Jewish quarter, where, as in Israel, I became more aware of my heritage. We visited an old Jewish cemetery where bodies had been interred over other bodies to fit into that cramped space. How deep did the graves go?

Perhaps my most significant experience was entering an old synagogue that displayed a concise history of the Jews and their never-ending struggle to survive prejudice, rampant antisemitism, and unimaginably cruel pogroms over the centuries. It was one thing to have read about that history, but to see it here, in this old, historic structure that had sheltered people who had been targeted in the Holocaust and for years before that, made it come alive, and made me part of it.

These stories were also my history. I felt an overwhelming sadness like a deep hole in the pit of my stomach. At the same time, there was anger. How could people be so cruel? And then the questions: if I'd been living in Prague, or another city in Germany or Austria or Poland, what would I have done? Would I have recognized what was going on? Would I have stayed? Would I have fought?

Those are questions that have become more relevant today with the rise of antisemitism in many countries in the world, including here in the United States. Could we go back to Canada? What is the tipping point? When do you know that something dire is about to take place? How do you know? How do people give up everything they know and everyone they care about in search of a better life – or, in the case of the Jews in Prague – a chance at survival?

In December 2015, Ellen and I embarked on a cruise on the Mekong River in Vietnam. Unlike the sleek, modern European cruise boats, this one was much smaller and made of wood, with a capacity of about sixty-five people, but it was only half full, which made the trip more intimate. While we found European culture different from that of North America, Asian culture was almost totally foreign. We were struck by the beauty of the country and the warmth and charm of the people, especially the children. I couldn't get enough of their smiling, giggling, winsome ways.

I'd read about the people – that they were friendly and welcoming, but experiencing it was an entirely different thing. We'd been at war with them, we'd bombarded them with agent orange, we'd destroyed so much of their land, and yet they welcomed us with deep sincerity and acceptance. We saw no hint of animosity. However, this was a communist government and our tour guide often chose his words carefully when talking about his country.

Part of my experience there was tied up in what I knew about the war, involving my ambivalence about the Marine Corps and my admiration for my father while also having protested our involvement there when I was a student. Looking at the war from a Vietnamese perspective allowed me to see the past in a more multi-dimensional way, especially after visiting the War Museum in Ho Chi Minh City.

I felt a little self-conscious, sad, and somewhat embarrassed to be an American.

Ellen had to walk out of the room that displayed photos of children maimed by agent orange. Some were horrendously affected by birth defects. All were harmed by the atrocity of war. These were facts U.S. citizens were not made aware of.

During the war, I thought I was well-informed, but I didn't know the history of Vietnam, that it had been invaded by China, then France, followed by Japan, and then the U.S., and all this time, for hundreds of years, the Vietnamese people had only wanted self-governance. Generations of outsiders had done their best to impose their rule on the Vietnamese. I hadn't known any of that until we arrived in the country.

I'd always wanted to go to Cuba, and we flew there from Miami in 2016, touring Havana and several other areas. I wanted to see the country for myself given the propaganda I'd been fed about the horror of communism. I was eager to experience what the Cubans had done under Castro. We probably didn't get the full picture – how can you when you are only in the country for a few weeks and the guides aren't as forthcoming as you want them to be? But I asked questions, pushing gently until our guide simply said. "It's complicated."

I certainly saw positive aspects of Cuba, including health care for everyone with generally excellent outcomes and free education right through university. There didn't appear to be limits on free speech, but the liberty to follow any profession – that didn't seem so obvious. It seemed to me that Cuba was more traditionally communist than Vietnam which appeared to have opened up more to capitalist enterprises. In Cuba, the government was in charge of almost everything. But the standard of living wasn't as bad as what I had imagined. I also had to keep in mind that if there were hardships, many of those were caused by the US embargo limiting any trade the country could do. And then there were the old cars from the fifties. Being a "car guy" they delighted me.

Vietnam, Cuba, Africa, Australia, Europe – all of them expanded my vision of the world and my place in it.

We didn't just explore foreign lands. We also went on quite a few road trips. One time we followed the Mississippi River from Minnesota right down to New Orleans. Another time, we drove through Quebec and the vast open wilds of northern Maine. Because I've always been fascinated with Native American history and culture, we drove from Denver north through Wyoming and Montana on what turned out to be one of our best road trips. I was particularly fascinated with the site of the Battle of Little Big Horn, spending hours walking the battlefield, trying to understand where the soldiers had attacked, their strategy, where they had died and where the indigenous people fell. We also went on road trips to all five national parks in Utah, Death Valley and Okefenokee Swamp in south Georgia.

Ellen and I attended all the annual CURE Ocular Melanoma patient meetings before Giuliana was born in 2014, and many after as well when we could care for Giuliana while Sara was busy with the conference. In fact, along with Becky, we helped Sara set up and run the first patient meeting she had in Boston in 2010.

After these meetings, we'd often embark on a road trip. After all, we were already away from home – why not take advantage of it? One time, when the meeting took place in Raleigh, North Carolina, we drove to the Outer Banks, a stunningly beautiful place with its charming villages and hundred plus miles of open seashore. A highlight of that trip was our visit to the site where the Wright brothers took their first flight. The excellent layout pinpointed the spot where the plane had taken off and where it had landed on its two initial flights. The image of that field is engraved on my mind.

It's clear to me that lifelong learning is important to me, effortlessly fueled by a curiosity that has been with me all my life. It may have gotten me into trouble a number of times (What would happen if I fired a rifle into a mattress?) but mostly, it has served me well. It guided me through an excellent education, and it has never allowed me to grow stagnant in my knowledge.

Curiosity is the driver that leads me to asking questions, getting to know how things work, and understanding how people work. Who are they? What do they do? And that would lead to more personal questions: What motivates me and what's behind the multiple parts of my personality? What fascinating facts and insights can others pass on to me? My father, of course, was also driven by curiosity. For both of us, it was an avenue to deep connections with people.

It was during the pandemic that Ellen and I traveled to five national parks in Utah., At that time, I was suffering from severe lower back pain and sciatica. I couldn't hike in Bryce Canyon. I could barely walk. One time, we drove highway 50 from Utah to Arizona, and for almost one hundred miles, we saw nothing – not a single building – except for the snaking ribbon of road, no sign that man had ever been there. We had a similar experience a few years later driving to Big Bend National Park in southern Texas. For long periods of time, we saw nobody.

I especially loved getting off the Interstate and taking the roads less traveled. Ellen worried about what might happen on those remote roads while I was drawn to the adventure.

You learn so much about yourself when you travel, especially if you face some adversity along the way. If everything doesn't go as planned, how do you react? Is it a disaster or is it a challenge that invites you to react nimbly and go with plan B – or possibly C, D, or even F? We couldn't do a river cruise in Hungary when the river overflowed and when we pivoted, we had a beautiful adventure.

I probably inherited some of my love of traveling from my parents. When my and Mary's children were growing up, my mother and dad took each of their four granddaughters on separate trips – special personal times with each girl that I'm sure was a formative experience for them. I think those trips probably influenced their own enjoyment of travel.

I believe my parents also influenced my fascination of other cultures. When Mary and I were growing up, the University of Denver hosted many international students, and several times a year, especially at Thanksgiving, they would call the university to invite one of them to dinner at our house. I was fascinated. One time we had a guest who was royalty in his country of The Gold Coast, now the Republic of Ghana.

By inviting people from different cultures, our parents were exposing us to different ways of thinking and being in the world. I remember my father pulling out an atlas on more than one occasion – "Show me where you're from."

That background at home stoked my curiosity, my love for travel, and hunger for learning, but not necessarily learning from a textbook. I wanted to gather knowledge firsthand, to experience a desert not by looking at photos in a magazine, but by kicking up the fine grains of sand with my boots and feeling the sun burning down on my shoulders. I didn't want to read about how a Sabra felt about his life in Jerusalem, I wanted to hear him tell me about walking down the narrow stone streets – and better yet, I wanted to walk beside him, listening to his stories.

CHAPTER 25

RETIREMENT?

I still operate Selig & Associates, the consultancy firm I started in 1996, although now I measure my work week in hours, not days. I'm proud of what I have accomplished. Hopefully, I've made a meaningful difference to the people and organizations I've worked with while earning a good living. I feel fortunate that the work that came to me was through excellent referrals. Clients also took me with them when they made moves to other companies. It's a good feeling, knowing you made a difference and had a positive impact, and people want to continue to work with you.

Almost daily, I receive an email in my inbox from McKinsey & Co. an American multinational strategy and management consulting firm that offers professional services to corporations, governments, and other organizations. They often hire the best and brightest from Harvard Business School. Stanford, Yale, and Wharton. Some of the research I receive is good and useful. A recent one discussed the dilemmas faced by many CEOs as they try to balance maintaining the company's current culture while also embracing new ideas and innovation. When I come across articles like this, I pass them on to my client list as a way of staying in touch as well as offering useful information.

Full retirement is not on my agenda. My work keeps me intellectually stimulated while satisfying my need to help others, and it's nice to still have an income. For me, a person who has always saved, one of the hardest things about shedding a major part of my workload was having to start dipping into my savings. Even though I might know intellectually that this is how it works as you get older, it's not how I was raised, and somehow, it doesn't feel quite right. There is satisfaction in watching a "nest egg" grow, a feeling entirely absent in seeing it dwindle, however slightly.

I may not work more than five or six hours a week now, but I think I do better work than ever. When I started consulting, I was younger than most of my clients, and consequently, often a bit intimidated. It isn't my age that has brought confidence, but the years of experience and the comfort of knowing who I am and the value of my contribution.

N.R. Narayana Murthy wrote, "The real power of money is the power to give it away." I believe that applies to more than money. I believe the real power of any knowledge and skill I have is the power to give it away. That is also the source of real satisfaction in any work you do – knowing you gave away what you know and have learned in hopes it will benefit others

Partly for that reason, I have been trying over the past eight plus years to understand and dialogue with Trump supporters. It started after becoming Facebook friends with a member of the Fairlane Club that I have belonged to since my dad passed on to me his 1967 Ford Fairlane convertible. The man was an ardent Trump supporter as were almost all his Facebook friends. Over the years I made a sincere effort to understand their lives, thoughts, and needs so I could comprehend their motivation. I also hoped I could help our country in however small a way.

When Trump came on the political scene in 2016, I followed the supporter's Facebook page, and still try to do the same with his fervent followers on Truth Social. In all these years, I've engaged only half a dozen people in real dialogue and a genuine exchange of ideas. My efforts have generally been met with name calling and unflattering assumptions about my beliefs and intelligence.

I've prided myself on posting and responding rationally and refraining from personal attacks. It has been an exercise in restraint as I've struggled not to react emotionally, something I've strived to do most of my adult life. It has also helped me achieve a greater understanding of the issues of our time.

In the last decade or more, I believe I have been doing a better job at giving, listening, and hearing, because I'm more comfortable in my own skin and more certain of the meaning and significance of my experience. I'm confident in my perceptions, and though my body is aging, I am not. In the movie, *The Mule,* Clint Eastwood said, "I try to get up and be productive, and don't let the old man in." That seems a pretty simple and fine way to go through each day. My correlated idea is to let the spontaneous, fun-loving, and challenging kid in me come out to play. Life needs some occasional gusto and spice.

Since 2000, an important part of my life has been volunteering with Hospice. My parents ingrained in me the value of volunteering, both by what they said, and in their deeds. I grew up knowing that making a difference was its own reward, and though I volunteered sporadically during my life, it wasn't until I signed up with hospice, that I became dedicated to a cause.

I chose Hospice because I wanted to prepare myself for my parents' death. I knew it was coming, not just intellectually, but also emotionally, and I thought Hospice would make me more comfortable with their passing.

I also believed and hoped that working with Hospice would make me a better person because if I was more in touch with my own death, perhaps I would live my life more consciously and congruently. I wanted the image I presented to the world to reflect accurately the person I was deep inside.

But I wasn't afraid of dying – not really. If I had any fears, it involved losing my parents, or Ellen, or my children. The longer I worked as a Hospice volunteer, the more I was at ease with death.

Of course, volunteering brought other unexpected rewards – a deep connection with some of the people I worked with, and the gift of giving to others.

Over the years, I visited perhaps two dozen people and grew close to four or five. Doug, one man I visited for about eighteen months, shared my interest in a number of things, including cars and the Old West. Our connection grew closer as I listened to his stories. One in particular struck me. He'd grown up with his grandparents who ran a filling station and café on the fabled Route 66. He had a myriad of memories from that time of the travelers who passed through and the incidents that occurred, including the occasion when an airplane ran out of gas and landed on the highway.

I was so fascinated with his tales, I was inspired to call the editor of a magazine called *Route 66*. He didn't exactly jump at the chance to interview Doug, but my persistence paid off and he eventually drove from New Mexico to Denver to do an interview. He published the story of Doug and his family, including photographs. Doug was thrilled, and because it meant so much to him, it also meant a lot to me that he had a written record – a tiny bit of immortality for him and his family.

The memory I have of some people still has the power to move me. Mary had had a difficult life: married twice to alcoholics and estranged from all her children. She was smart and had wanted a college education, but was too poor to afford it. At the end of her life, she was alone and it broke my heart. I wish I could have done more to make her feel better about her life. I think she derived some small pleasure from the times I pushed her wheelchair up and down the halls of the nursing home and outside so she could feel sunshine on her face. I gave her as much as I could. I just wish I could have given more.

I was always careful about who I chose to visit as a Hospice volunteer. I knew I would do my best and bring the most value to someone I could talk with and connect to. All my life, I've been curious about people, asking questions and drawing them out. I brought that same eagerness to Hospice, and while those who were dying had someone to share their stories with, I received the great reward of hearing them.

I hope that everyone I interacted with felt that someone was bearing witness to their life and story. I hope they felt seen and heard.

We all know that our time on earth is limited, but when we can see the finish line in front of us, we deserve to be heard.

Some people I spent time with wanted to talk about dying while others did not. The Hospice philosophy is perfect: go where the person wants to go. I hope I was there for them and that I was good at bearing witness.

When I look back on my life, I sometimes wonder how it would have been if I'd followed my heart and not my head. I grew up knowing I had to earn a living and be responsible, but deep inside there lurked a bit of a rebel aching with wanderlust. What would my life have been like if I'd moved to Alaska in the sixties? I didn't have the psychology to do it, but the curiosity and love of nature were there. Interestingly, I remember my dad saying once that he'd always wanted a ranch in an isolated spot surrounded by wildlife, rolling foothills leading to snow-capped peaks, and big skies, but with all the modern conveniences.

I'd wanted a place in the mountains for years, and in 1997, Ellen and I had saved enough to buy a small A-frame cabin in Estes Park. For a few years, we rented it out until we no longer needed the income it generated. In 2009, we tore it down, replacing it with a house that is our getaway. It sits on 2.5 acres, and though it's in a rural neighborhood, it's still a refuge where I wish I could spend more time. I hope it stays in the family for generations.

A big, important part of our family is our granddaughter, Giuliana. She was born March 19, 2014. Words can't express the delight we felt and the delight she is – and was, from the moment she was born.

One of Ellen's family members recently said, "Grandchildren are the dessert of life."

Absolutely.

I was enamored with Sara and I was equally enamored with Becky, but I was blown away by Giuliana. Maybe this feeling of absolute unconditional love is about my age and being a grandparent who isn't responsible in the way that a parent is, but for whatever reason, I adore her. Perhaps, in some way, Giuliana represents an opportunity to make up for the mistakes I made with my own children, and the regrets I have about that.

In the time I have left, I want to do my best with Sara, Becky, and Ellen to make amends for everything I did wrong. I can't change the past, but I want to be better now at showing my love, gratitude, and appreciation to these very special women. I want to be more attentive and caring. I want to leave no doubt in their minds how I feel, and more importantly, how I have always felt – every moment of every day, even though I haven't always shown it. I wish I had.

From the beginning, I bonded with Giuliana skin to skin. I have pictures of me sleeping with her on my bare chest.

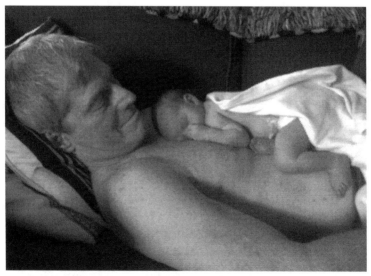

Figure 18 Giuliana and me. 2014

The photo doesn't show the fullness of the peace that washed over me at times like that. The bond I felt with her from the first day continues to deepen. Today, at age ten, she is a warm, sensitive, compassionate, thoughtful, smart, athletic kid – beautiful inside and out. I hope I live long enough to witness her maturing and growing into herself.

Figure 19 Ellen, me, Becky, Giuliana, and Sara. Florida 2018

Giuliana and I love to play. Her favorite game is "Tickle Monster," which is pretty much exactly what it sounds like. I act like a fool, of course. It won't be long before she won't want to play it anymore, but recently when we visited in Boston, one of the first things she said was, "Boppa, I want to play tickle monster." It's one of the highlights of my life to tickle her up her legs and ribs, kissing her neck all the while, listening to her giggling.

Ellen doesn't generally behave as silly as I do, but not long ago, that shifted. Sara, Ellen, Giuliana and I were leaving a restaurant and passed a fire hydrant on the sidewalk. Knowing Giuliana loved dogs, Ellen lifted her leg. Minutes later, she got into the back seat of the car, lowered the window in front of Giuliana and started panting and barking, her paws (hands) held up like a puppy's. Giuliana, who adores dogs, laughed and laughed. I laughed so hard I couldn't stop, even after getting behind the wheel and pulling out into the road. Tears blurred my vision so I could barely see the road.

Ellen's sharp and droll humor doesn't surface as much as my ironic and occasional slapstick style, but when she lets it out, it can bring the house down. Sometime in the early eighties, we hosted a dinner party at our house for eight or ten people. We brought out the good silver we'd received as a wedding gift, the "good" dishes, and the linen napkins. Ellen was coming into the room from the kitchen with a serving platter when one of the men, who was a good friend, picked up a silver spoon and said, "Ellen, this spoon has a spot on it."

Ellen set down the platter, took the spoon from him, spit on it, wiped it with her hands, and gave it back to him. We still laugh at the memory.

Ellen likes to have fun and has given me some wonderful surprise parties. The first was my thirtieth in 1973, just before we got married. It was also a celebration for receiving my doctorate. The afternoon of the party, she told me we had to go to the house she nominally still shared with her roommates. However, I had a bad case of diarrhea and wasn't feeling at all well.

"I don't want to go," I said.

"Andy, it's a party. We have to go."

I had no idea it was for me, and reluctantly I let her drag me there. Ellen had worked hard at creating a wonderful experience for me, and meanwhile, I kept running to the bathroom while trying to be present and look like I was enjoying myself.

We always had a lot of friends, but they weren't all part of one particular group, so the people at the party meant a lot to Ellen and me, but most didn't know each other. Consequently, the party never really gelled. Neither did my insides.

In 1983, a neighbor helped Ellen organize a surprise for my fortieth birthday. He came over to the house on the Saturday afternoon of my birthday. "Hey, Selig," he said. "Let's get stoned."

That seemed like a fine idea. We toked up and pretty soon, another friend joined us and we piled into someone's car and drove to a bar in one of Denver's more disreputable neighborhoods. Along the way, they bought a birthday cake topped with a nude woman decoration that they carried into the bar. After a couple of beers, and eating most of the cake, we got back into the car and drove to the local community pool where we were members. Walking in, about fifty or sixty people shouted "Happy Birthday!"

Ellen had pulled it off. I was massively surprised, and I had a great time until, while playing a vigorous round of volleyball, I zipped under the net and tackled one of my friends. During the ensuing brief wrestling match, I broke a toe. It doesn't sound like much, but it hurt something awful. I found a chair, eased myself into it, and elevated my throbbing toe. My dad spotted me and strode over. "Andy, Ellen went to a lot of trouble and expense for this party and you're over here sitting on your ass. Get up and enjoy it!"

"Dad," I said. "My toe really hurts."

"So? Buck up. Be a man. Be grateful and enjoy the party."

And I did, despite the sore toe.

I returned the favor by throwing a party for Ellen on her fortieth. I rented a Native American art gallery near downtown Denver – a super space on two levels with a balcony overlooking the main room. Sara, who was thirteen and who I swore to secrecy, helped me clean, tidy, and decorate the day before. I hired a band and invited all our friends – probably about a hundred guests.

I convinced her we were going out to dinner with another couple. As we were about to drive by the gallery, our friend, who was in real estate, said he wanted to stop to look at the gallery with an eye to purchasing it. We got out of the car and walked in to a deafening chorus of Happy Birthday!

She was completely flabbergasted, not only by the delight and joy of seeing all her friends, but by the fact that I actually managed to pull it off.

In the summer of 2023, Ellen and I flew to Maui to celebrate our fiftieth anniversary and my eightieth birthday. We'd been to Hawaii when Ellen was pregnant with Sara, and years later we brought both girls to the islands. They were great trips, but this one was just for the two of us and it was special.

We snorkeled, took long walks on the beach, sat on the sand where turtles lumbered past us, hiked along an idyllic coastline trail, and drove on empty winding roads through lush tropical forests as we reminisced about the past fifty years.

We spent time in Lahaina, the capital city that would be destroyed by a wildfire only months later. We were enchanted by the old town with a history that went back hundreds of years. We ate dinner on a second-floor balcony there, looking down at the square where tourists wandered aimlessly while vendors called to each other and golden plumeria perfumed the air.

Figure 20 Ellen and me. Maui for our 50th and my 80th. 2023

CHAPTER 26

REFLECTIONS

I've had to dig deep inside to write this book. I have examined not only my actions, but also my thoughts and feelings at the deepest level. So how can I summarize who I was, who I grew into, and who I am today?

As hard as I try to understand myself, I do not – not at the level I would like to. Like all humans, I am a multifaceted being. How can I put such complexities into words? Still, if you're reading this, I want you to know me, so I shall try.

I value human connection and want very much to be close to others, especially those I love. And yet, too often I behave in ways that drive away the people I love the most. I'm much less impatient, judgmental, intolerant, controlling and self-centered than I was in the past, but still more than I would like to be. I see both sides of me: the loving and compassionate as well as the more judgmental and intolerant side. Ellen tells me she is impressed with the extent to which I've overcome my negative, destructive instincts, and with the fact that I've made such a big effort in those areas. She points out that many people aren't willing or able to really look at themselves and change. Her encouragement helps me feel better about myself.

What I really want and crave is kind, loving, fun, and stimulating interactions and experiences.

Native Americans call it the good wolf and the bad wolf. The one that grows strong is the one you feed. Naturally, I want to feed the good wolf. I'm getting better at that and I'm much more aware when I start tossing scraps to the bad wolf, but I still slip more than I would like to.

I am proud of certain aspects of who I am. I work hard and when I set my mind to something, no matter the challenge or obstacles, I don't give up. I have the same dogged determination if I want to understand something, whether it's a person, a mechanism, or a concept. If I set my mind to it, I will come to a place of comprehension. I'm proud of my values. Based on how I was raised, I value being compassionate, making life better for as many as I can, continually improving myself and practicing the art of making do with less. I know that material things are just that – things. However, I was raised to respect and take care of things, so that's still a focus. But what is most important is the people I love and my relationships with them.

I'm an emotional person. Tears come easily. Sometimes I try, mostly unsuccessfully, to hide them, afraid I'll be teased, but I am deeply moved by other's feelings and by those who inspire me. When I was watching the 2024 Democratic National Convention, I was deeply touched by the vision of a future of caring for and helping each other. When Tim Walz was speaking and a camera picked up his teen-age son in the audience, weeping as he listened to his father speak, I simply broke down. I felt that momentous moment he was experiencing with his dad as profoundly as though it was my own.

Sometimes my tears come unexpectedly, and while I know it's an authentic part of who I am, I'm also embarrassed.

I feel safest with Ellen, and yet there are still times I act like a jerk with her, rather than being vulnerable. Being vulnerable is key to successful relationships and to a rich, meaningful life. The positive ripple effects of being comfortable with vulnerability cut wide and deep. Sometimes, I find it disheartening that I'm still not the "better man" I want to be. I'm not as much of a jerk anymore and not for as long a time, but still…

For more than fifty years, Ellen has had my back. Once I wrote, "Home is not a place, it's being with Ellen."

I could write that every day, because it's true. My love and life with Ellen was not made in heaven, but in real life, with hurt, frustration, impatience, anger, loneliness, disappointment, and sadness, but also with a fundamental, unbroken foundation of connection, understanding, and caring.

I want to be genuinely vulnerable with her all the time. You'd think that at my age – eighty-plus, I'd have outgrown the petty jerk, but will I ever? Will any of us ever transcend the human condition? Can we ever rise above our lifelong reactions to disappointment and frustration? Hopefully we continue to improve.

One thing writing this book has taught me is that life is a process of refining and updating our stories to help make our lives coherent and meaningful.

What is the storyline running through my life? A will to accomplish something. A desire to help others. A wish to be liked and respected. To be seen as smart, fun, and unpredictable. I have always been curious and have continually strived to be a better person. I've also tried to continue to bring fun and some pot-stirring into my life and into the lives of those around me. Much of life is serious, and it's better managed by finding ways to have fun, laugh, and bring out that ever-present little kid in all of us.

In my practice, if I was feeling blue, I'd listen even more carefully, acutely conscious of anything I could do to help. Over the years, I've worked hard at making this practice a reality in my personal life as well.

In this memoir, I've had an opportunity to look back on my life in a way many people never do, in what I feel is a combination of pride and regret. I certainly have a sense of accomplishment, but also a feeling of things undone and things I wish I had done better. I sometimes think of all the different lives I could have led. What If I'd gone to Alaska? What if we had stayed in Vancouver? What if I'd become a car mechanic? What if I had taken a different path?

I remember the movie, *Groundhog Day* where Bill Murray woke up each morning on the same day in the same place, and just one little thing he did differently changed the course of his life.

What if?

EPILOGUE

In this last year, 2024, I've been fortunate to find Goody Lindley, someone who is a great listener, who asks good questions, who is empathetic, who has held a mirror up to me, and has helped me articulate my story. It has been a wonderful gift to have a chance to reflect on my life.

This unique and terrific experience has helped me wrap up my story. I am left with a sense of completion. If I die tomorrow, I sense that I am leaving something important behind – and part of that is a tribute to those who paved the way for me and from whom I learned so much.

My life has benefitted from the interest I took in my ancestors. What I learned from them and about them, helped me understand where I came from and who I came from. What I learned helped me understand myself and encouraged me to strive toward my goals as they did..

Everything I learned and extrapolated from that knowledge, has been a positive factor in my life. In many ways, I've tried to emulate the positive aspects of those who came before me, and, through them, find my place in the scheme of life. They have given me a sense of belonging and a concept of my place in the world.

By sharing my life, openly and honestly with my children and grandchildren and the generations to come, and by including what I know of my parents and grandparents, I hope to benefit them in some way.

If I've included useful information or even advice, they can choose to take to heart what makes sense to them. I hope they find some encouragement in knowing that others have met obstacles on their paths that they have managed to overcome.

Knowing about what my ancestors endured, has, at times, helped me pick myself up when I've been down.

To my granddaughter, Giuliana, other descendants I will never know, and anyone else who reads this, I want to offer a few words of counsel.

Figure out who you are. Be pleased and grateful that you are who you are, warts and all. Accept who you are, but know you are a work in progress. Always strive to be a better person and to be the best of who you are. Take risks, face and attack those things that intimidate you if they are things you really want to do. Confidence comes from pushing out of your comfort zone and proving to yourself that you can do it. But also keep in mind that who you are is the core of your being – and that is wonderful indeed.

Trust yourself. Have confidence in your intuition about what you want to do with your life. Trust that you know what is most important to you.

Giuliana, being your grandfather has been a highlight of my life. And to those who come after me, know that I wish I could know you.

ACKNOWLEDGMENTS

This book would never have been conceived, much less written, without the nudging and persuasiveness of my daughter, Sara. It would not have been written in any fashion, much less in my voice and in a flowing and hopefully interesting and captivating way, without the skill of Goody Lindley. Goody's writing abilities are only surpassed by her compassion, question asking prowess, skill in humanizing my shortcomings so I could be honest and vulnerable, and her ongoing encouragement that our effort would be meaningful to my family and even possibly to others. Finally, but equally significant, I could never have written this book without Ellen, whose never-ending caring, psychological support, ability to hold up a mirror for me to see myself as I am rather than as I thought I was, and her fact checking, all of which has kept me going, and from whom I've gotten the bulk of my courage to own up more to my humanity and vulnerabilities.

APPENDIX

Dad's Obituary

Leon Selig was born on June 20, 1909, in New York City, and grew up in St. Louis, MO. He consistently set high goals for himself, first evident by becoming and Eagle Scout. He began working at the May Company as a stock boy and moved to Denver in 1936. He worked his way up, becoming a successful independent and astute businessman in retail, real estate, and investment. Leon married Emily Mayer in 1938. He proudly volunteered to serve in the Marine Corps in 1943 at the age of 34, later volunteering for the USO. He was dedicated to community service and served in many capacities and boards, including the Planned Parenthood local and national boards. He was well respected and asked to remain on the Auraria Community Center Board during the turbulent 1960s. Leon and Emily traveled extensively later in life and introduced their grandchildren to the appreciation of other cultures and peoples. He was devoted tohis family and inculcated in them his strong values of hard work, loyalty, humility and service to others.

"Big Daddy" was loved by many, especially his wife Emily, of 65 years, his children, grandchildren and great grandson, Andy, Ellen, Sara, and Becky Selig, Mary and Sunny Justice, Aimee, Steve, and Max Lundt.

A memorial service will be held on Wednesday, April y at 1:00 PM at Fairmount Little Ivy Chapel. In lieu of flowers donations may be made to Planned Parenthood or Hospice of Metro Denver.

OBITUARY

Leon 'Big Daddy' Selig learned values as a World War II Marine

By Jeff Smith
ROCKY MOUNTAIN NEWS

Leon "Big Daddy" Selig attributed his values and disciplined approach to his service in the Marine Corps in San Diego during World War II — a service he volunteered for at the age of 34, his family said.

"He was proud of that and would have liked to have gone overseas," said his wife of 65 years, Emily Selig.

His son, Andy, added: "He said he loved every day (of being in the Marine Corps). Everything was a challenge he wanted to meet head-on" — even cleaning toilets with a toothbrush.

Mr. Selig, the grandson of a German immigrant mining engineer and a successful real estate investor in Denver, died April 4 with his family at his side. He was 94.

His daughter, Mary, said her father was called "Big Daddy" because of his role as the family patriarch.

"He was the big boss," Mary said, adding that he commanded respect through a combination of love and sternness. "He loved unconditionally, but that didn't mean you didn't have to hold your own and do the right thing."

Mr. Selig grew up in St. Louis, started at the May Co. department store chain as a stock boy and moved to Denver in 1936.

He was an on-the-road salesman when he started buying houses and fixing them up on the side. Eventually, Mr. Selig built some apartment buildings in Denver and ran them.

"I helped him do the maintenance work," Andy said. "He was hands-on. He believed anything worth doing was worth doing right."

Mary said her father was very proud of Emily, who is well-known for her decades-long work as a volunteer at Children's Hospital in Denver.

Emily said her late husband also had a strong sense of community, serving on the board of Planned Parenthood and spending much of his time at the Auraria Community Center, one of a half-dozen community centers in Denver at the time.

Around the early 1960s, Mr. Selig and another board member raised $30,000 — enough money to build a community center in the Hispanic neighborhood at West 10th Avenue and Mariposa Street.

Andy, now 60, recalls going to a board meeting when Hispanic leaders decided they no longer wanted Anglos on the board. "The upshot was that there was one Anglo they wanted to stay on the board, and that was my dad," Andy said.

Mr. Selig was outgoing and the type who wanted to know all he could about other people but didn't really talk about himself, his children said.

He was active well into his late years. In fact, the family celebrated his 90th birthday at a dude ranch in Colorado — with both Leon and Emily riding horses just as they had done in their early years.

When the staff presented Mr. Selig with a gag gift of horse manure in a cowboy boot box at the end of the week, he just threw back his head and laughed hard at the joke.

Great-grandson Max, now 2 years old, recently had become the light of Mr. Selig's life. Little Max would climb on Mr. Selig's lap and "seemed to pick up on my father's fragility," Andy said.

A memorial service was held April 7 at Fairmount Little Ivy Chapel.

My Mother's Obituary

Emily Mayer Selig was born on August 13, 1916, in Denver, Colorado, first child to Aimee and Adolph Mayer. She was very proud of her Colorado heritage and passed on stories from her grandfather Leopold Mayer, who came to Denver in 1859 in a covered wagon. She attended East High School and Skidmore College. Emily married Leon Selig in 1938, and had two children, Andy and Mary. She began volunteering at Children's Hospital at the age of 12, with her mother, and continued, based on her philosophy of love begets love, until she was 90. She held thousands of babies, some of whom died in her arms. Although a very humble person, she received The 9 Who Care award. Throughout her lifetime, she also passionately volunteered in numerous other organizations. Emily lived the Golden Rule, striving always to be kind, giving, tolerant and loving. She drew people of all ages and walks of life to her because of her sincere concern for and interest in them, her grace, and her ability to accept life as it unfolds. She traveled extensively with Leon and her family, introducing their children and grandchildren to different people and cultures, the values of acceptance and diversity, and the importance of family. Emily (Grammommie to her grandchildren) was loved and admired by those who knew her, especially her late husband, Leon, her children, grandchildren and great grandchildren; Mary Justice, Sunny and Joshua Meyer, Aimee, Steve, Max and Eliot Lundt, Andy and Ellen Selig, Becky Selig, Sara Selig and Gregg Stracks. A memorial service will be held at 1:00 pm Tuesday May 13, 2008 at the Fairmount Ivy Chapel. In lieu of flowers, please make donations to the charity of your choice. Published in the Denver Newspaper Agency on 5/11/2008

My maternal grandmother Aimee Levi Mayer's Obituary

Mrs. Aimee L. Mayer, 77, of 1515 E. 9th Ave., longtime Denver resident and widow of Adolph Mayer, prominent Denver businessman, died last week following a brief illness at the Rose Hospital.

Rabbi Joseph Goldman, officiated at her last rites, spoke of her tremendous capacity to love and be loved. "Her love of humanity, of her children and grandchildren, can be likened to that of the Prophet Hosea. Her kindness and good deeds touched and enriched the lives of so many. She was a gracious woman who had an especially warm smile. As a rabbi, I share the pain with her family over her loss."

Mrs. Mayer was born in Shreveport, La. She came to Denver as a young woman and attended Colorado Woman's College. Her husband, whom she married in 1914, died in 1960.

Mrs. Mayer was one of the pioneer members of the board of the Denver Children's Hospital, and at one time worked for the National Jewish Hospital. She was a member of Temple Micah.

Mrs. Mayer is survived by a son, Adolph (Bud) Mayer, director of public relations at D.U.; two daughters, Mrs. Leon Selig and Mrs. Albert Ambrose, both of Denver; five grandchildren and a sister, Mrs. Edith Wallbrunn of Denver. Interment was bat Fairmount.

Denver Furniture Man Dies

Adolph Mayer, prominent Denver furniture dealer, died Saturday in a Denver rest home. He was 86.

Born Feb. 22, 1874, in San Luis, Colo., he was reared in Saguache on his father's ranch. He attended public schools there, and later the present Notre Dame University in South Bend, Ind., when it was a military prep school.

He was married Dec. 28, 1914, to the former Aimie Levy in Denver. They lived at 1515 E. Ninth ave.

He came to Denver as a young man and was co-founder of the American Furniture Co. He later opened his own store, the Mayer Furniture Co., at 1625 California st. He retired in 1929.

He was a member of Columbine Lodge of the Masons, and Congregation Micah.

Surviving, in addition to his wife, are a son, Adolph Bud Jr., director of public relations at Denver University; two daughters, Mrs. Emily Selig and Mrs. Barbara Ambrose; a brother, Sam; and five grandchildren, all of Denver.

Funeral arrangements are pending, and will be directed by Olinger's Mortuary.

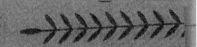

Adolph Mayer

Adolph Mayer Sr., 86, retired Denver furniture executive, died Saturday at the Valley Manor Rest Home, 4601 E. Asbury Ave. He lived at 1515 E. 9th Ave.

At the turn of the century, Mayer helped found the American Furniture Co. here. He remained with this firm until 1925, when he established a furniture store bearing his name. He operated that store until retiring in 1929.

Born Feb. 22, 1874 in San Luis, Colo., Adolph Sr. attended public schools in nearby Saguache.

Mayer married Amie Levy here Dec. 28, 1914.

He was a founder of the Sons of Colorado, an organization whose members are pioneers or are related to such persons, and was a member of the Columbine Masonic Lodge, B'nai B'rith and Congregation Micah.

Survivors in addition to his wife include a son, Adolph (Bud) Mayer Jr., public relations director for the University of Denver; two daughters, Mrs. Emily Selig and Mrs. Barbara Ambrose, both of Denver, and five grandchildren.

Services will be announced later.

My maternal great grandfather Obituary

Jewish Banker and Merchant Had Picturesque Career.

Leopold Mayer, pioneer banker and merchant, passed away in Denver at the home of his son, Samuel B. Mayer, 910 St. Paul street, at the age of eighty-eight.

Born in Alsace-Lorraine, he was eleven years old when he landed in New York City. After staying there a short time, he went to Lafayette, Ind., and there heard of the gold discoveries in Colorado. With several friends, he came to Denver and shortly thereafter went into business at 15th and Market street. In 1880 he engaged in the cattle business at Saguache, Colo., where he later opened a bank. He was vice-president of the bank at the time of his death.

Mr. Mayer served as representative to the state legislature from Saguache County.

He retired from active business two years ago and came to Denver to make his home with his sons. Three sons are surviving him, Louis Mayer, Adolph of the Mayer Furniture Co. and Sam Mayer.

———◆———

Jerusalem (J. T. A.)—A Palestine section at the International Hygiene Exhibition in Dusseldorf, Germany, will be arranged, according to a report of the Zionist Executive here.

The exhibition will be opened the beginning of May.

My maternal great grandmother's obituary

Died, in Saguache, Colorado, on Wednesday morning, Feb. 3d, 1886, BARBARA SOLOMON, wife of Leopold Mayer, aged about thirty-three years.

The deceased was the third child of Philip and Bertha Solomon, and was born at Lafayette, Indiana. She was married to Leopold Mayer on Jan. 9, 1873, at Homer, Illinois, and accompanied her husband to his home at this place, where she resided up to the time of her death. Four children have blessed their union: Adolph, aged twelve; Louis, aged nine; Samuel, aged six; Frederic, aged three years.

The deceased was a lovely woman, and was a joy and comfort in her home, and a blessing to the community in which she dwelt. Kind and devoted, her every thought seemed to center about the family circle, her husband and four lovely boys, and no sacrifice seemed to her too great in their behalf. She was a person possessed of sterling qualities, and her quiet unassuming manner, gave her great influence among her extended circle of friend; but it was never used to the discomfort of her associates. Her goodness of heart led her to many acts of charity, and her memory will long be cherished by those less fortunate than was she in this world's stores.

In this, his terrible bereavement, Mr. Mayer is compelled to part with the companion of his choice; and the loss is felt the more keenly, because she who was the light and joy of his home was so suddenly called hence. The children have lost a loving and affectionate mother, and a wise counsellor,—one who early sought to impress on their young minds the necessity of living moral and upright lives. To the affectionate husband, and the doting children, the sympathy of the entire community is extended.

The immediate cause of her death was heart disease, in the form of valvular lesion, from which she has suffered for some years, and which, at last, baffled the skill of eminent physicians. Last week Mr. Mayer caused a telegram to be sent to Denver for a physician, and Dr. W. S. Craig, an eminent physician of that city came on Wednesday in answer to the summons. After a careful examination of the patient, he informed the sorrowing husband that while his companion might partially recover, he must be prepared for the worst at any moment. The treatment as employed by Dr. W. F. Bogart (who had been the physician for a few days), was fully endorsed. The patient seemed to rally, and an a marked improvement was visible, until early Wednesday morning when the disease took its fatal turn, and the spirit of the sufferer was ushered into rest.

The remains were placed in a sealed casket and, on Thursday morning, was taken to Denver for interment. The remains were accompanied by the bereaved husband and the two oldest sons. The funeral services are to be held at the Emmanuel Synagogue, on Sunday, and the body laid to rest in the Riverside burial ground.

Article about the Leopold and Barbara Solomon
Mayer family in Colorado Territorial Families 1981

Colorado Families:
A Territorial Heritage

Compiled and Published by
The Colorado Genealogical Society, Inc.
Denver, Colorado
1981

(Denver: Colorado Genealogical Society, 1981)

became acquainted with Aunt Jo in Paris during World War II and loved her dearly. She also gave me five sterling silver forks that had belonged to her mother with the initial 'M' on them. They had been bought at Gotteslabens, the first jewelry store in Denver."

Josephine took care of her mother during her long illness prior to her death in 1896 and shortly after, when her father became ill in SLC, she went there and cared for him until his death in 1892.

3 ALBERT MARION was born on 18 Jun 1867 in Denver where he was a stock broker. He was married in San Francisco for a short time. During the Crash of 1929 he lost everything, the shock of which effected him mentally. He spent periods of his last years in various hospitals including one in Colo Spgs where he died at the age of 63, and was buried at Mt Olivet Cem in Denver 20 Aug 1930. A dear person through it all, he was loved and respected by the family and everyone who knew him. Albert had a son, Ted, brought up partly by Angele (Marion) Scherrer, then became ward of Josephine Marion, accompanied her to France. He lived in San Francisco and contributed to his father's support in later years.

Contributors: May (Scherrer) Eckhardt, Helen (Mattingly) Scherrer, Irma (Scherrer) Williamson

LEOPOLD AND BARBARA (SOLOMON) MAYER

LEOPOLD MAYER was born in Alsace Lorraine in Sep 1839. He married in Lafayette, Tippecanoe Co, Ind c1870 (1) Barbara Solomon born in Ind in 1853, daughter of a German immigrant. She died at Saguache, Saguache Co, Colo sometime after 1885 of typhoid fever and it is thought to have been buried in Denver. (Riverside Cem has a Mrs B Mayer, age 33, died 6 Feb 1886). About a year later, Leopold married (2) Pauline Schloesman who was born in Illinois in Oct 1853 and died in Denver 1923. Leopold died 6 Feb 1926 at the home of his son, Samuel, at 910 St Paul, Denver. Both are buried at Riverside.

According to his great grandson, Andrew Selig, Leopold landed in New York at the age of nine with only one relative in the US, an aunt. He was then taken to Lafayette where he sold matches on street corners for a living. He was deprived of an education because he was compelled to work at many different things until he was about 18. Then on a Mississippi river boat he made his way to St Louis and from there he traveled to Leavenworth, Kan, the "jumping off" place to the West. Leopold found a man who was ready to start for the Pikes Peak region with several ox teams. This meant walking the entire distance of about 600 miles, hoping, if they were lucky, to make 10 miles a day. The men walked alongside the wagons the entire distance and the trip took them a good 60 days. They had to endure many hardships, always fearful of Indian attacks or buffalo stampedes.

Their route took them to a point near Cherry Cr where they found good water and grazing, and following the creek they came upon the fork of Cherry Cr and the Platte Riv. At this point there was a settlement, mostly of Indians. There were actually two small towns in this area, one was known as St Charles and the other as Auraria. This later became the present site of Denver. All this took place about 1859. Some time later Leopold bought two lots for $10 each. After remaining in Denver a short time, he decided to go up to the placer mine diggings in the mountains around Georgetown. A good portion of this territory was named Gregory Gulch after the first man who found gold there. When Leopold wanted to leave Colo and sell his two lots, nobody would buy them because he had no title although this was a common thing in those days. He learned of the building of the UPRR through Wyo and Ut and decided to follow the building of the railroad. Every 10 miles the men would put up a temporary town and then move it when 10 miles of track were completed. They joined with the railroad from the west at Promontory, Ut, and there a golden spike was driven. Leopold witnessed this great happening on 10 May 1868, an important historical event in railroad history. He then returned to Denver and purchased a team of mules and a covered wagon and began delivering merchandise. His sales route consisted of making a trip through S Park down to the Arkansas Riv and then into the San Luis Valley. Then he circled back by way of Pueblo and Colo Spgs into Denver. After making many of these trips he finally settled in San Luis, the oldest town in Colo, first called Culebra (Spanish for "snake," after the Culebra Riv which winds through the countryside). It was next known as Plaza Del Medis, Spanish for "center village" because of its geographical location to San Pedro. Leopold then engaged in the mercantile business with Otto Mears, known as the pathfinder who became famous in the building and development of southern Colo.

Leopold was elected to the first city council of Denver in 1861 and was selected to go to Colo City where the capital of the Terr was established in 1861. In 1888 he also represented Saguache in the State House of Representatives. A bill was introduced to make an appropriation to purchase new chandeliers for the House chambers. After considerable debate, one of the members who opposed the appropriation said he might support it if the House would adopt an amendment which he would propose. This amendment was to buy a male and female chandelier and raise their own! In 1864 the capital was moved to Mtn City, now known as Golden, and remained there only about a year and a half before being moved to Denver.

At about this time the Indians became an increasing problem and the govt established a fort S of Alamosa, known as Fort Garland originally named Fort Massachusetts. It was about 15 miles from San Luis and Leopold received a contract from the US govt to furnish beef to the soldiers there. This meant the raising, buying and fattening of beef and, being friendly with the Indian agent, he found it to his advantage to raise his cattle on the reservation. There was very good feed there and he had the protection of the fort nearby. However on one of the Indian raids of the reservation, perhaps by an opposing tribe, the Indians drove the cattle out, took their hides and left the carcasses to waste. Naturally the loss was terrible and Leopold put in a claim to the govt for the loss. After about 50 yrs, the courts threw out the claim, stating that he had no right on the Indian reservation with his cattle, even though this right had been given to him by the chief of the reservation.

Leopold then went back to Ind, was married, and brought his bride back across the plains by ox team. In 1874 about three families of white people lived in San Luis. Later the Mayer family moved to a small community to the north called Saguache, named after Saguache Cr (a Ute Indian word meaning "blue earth" or "water at the blue earth"). The first settlement was known as Milton which was originally located about one mile away from the present site. The land there was marshy so the town was moved and some bldgs were also actually moved in the process. When their oldest child was about 12 yrs old, Barbara became ill with typhoid fever, a common deadly killer in those days, and after a few days of illness she died. Leopold left his two babies with a kind neighbor and set off with his older sons on a bitter cold Jan day to take his wife's coffin to Villa Grove, the nearest railroad station about 20 miles away. At the station he put his wife's body on the train to be buried in Denver. They rode in an open wagon drawn by a team of horses, the two boys in the back with the coffin covered by a blanket. They cried with cold and fear as Leopold drove and wondered how to care for four motherless children in the small, raw pioneer town. He succeeded well, however, and three of them grew to adulthood and produced descendants to carry on Leopold's spirit that, in Andrew's words, "cried out for adventure and the chance to make a fortune with bare hands or go broke. That spirit demanded courage. It meant hardship and disappointment which were expected and tossed aside when they appeared. The spirit meant life in the 'raw', yet no one ever wanted to 'go back home'."

Leopold opened the Saguache County Bank, one of the first in the Rockies, and served as its first pres. He was also involved in ranching and in the mercantile business with Isaac Gotthelp until he retired in 1924. In 1891 Leopold built a house on the corner of 17th and Ogden in Denver (940 17th). He was one of the founders of Temple Emmanuel. [Bib: Sons, 1 #9, II #1]

Chn of Leopold and Barbara (Soloman) Mayer

2   i   Adolph, b 22 Feb 1874
3   ii   Louis H, b Feb 1877
4   iii   Samuel B, b 16 Aug 1879
     iv   Frederick, b 1882 Saguache; d 9 Feb 1891; bur Riverside Cem, Denver

2   ADOLPH MAYER was born 22 Feb 1874 in San Luis, Costilla Co. He was married in Denver 28 Dec 1914 to Aimee Levy born 2 Feb 1888 in Shreveport, Caddo Co, La. Adolph died 5 Mar 1960 and Aimee 4 Apr 1965, both in Denver and they are buried in Fairmount Cem.

According to his daughter, Emily, Adolph was the first Anglo born in San Luis and he grew up in Saguache. Among many of the experiences of which he told his grandson, Andrew, was the one of his very first day at school. Children were not required by law to go to sch and many had to help their parents, or were living in an outlying dist where there were no

schools. Adolph, at the age of seven and living in Saguache attended only a very short time. This school was a large room in an adobe structure converted into an open sch room, while the back part of the bldg was used for a jail. The sch had no desks but a bench around the wall to sit on. Adolph remembers that he had a strong urge to go to sch. On this day he was sitting by a boy who was very much older than he; the boy stuck a pin in Adolph's leg and Adolph hollered. The punishment for yelling was to stay in at recess. When he went home at noon his father asked him how sch was and he replied, "I've had enough; I'm not going back there!" He remembered in his class a tall Indian called "Big Boy" who was 30 yrs old and was trying to learn his ABCs.

When Adolph was about 11 he had the unusual experience of seeing a hanging in Saguache. Naturally this created a great deal of excitement but very few people had any desire at all to witness such an event. On the morning of this occurrence, Adolph started for the courthouse yard and much to his surprise he was met by his father who might have been a little suspicious or it might have been a coincidence. Nevertheless, he asked Adolph where he was going, and Adolph answered, "Going to the hanging." His father then said, "You're a little off your beat; you go right back on the path that leads you to school." When Leopold was out of sight, Adolph went to the execution. It was the sheriff's duty to spring the trap, but it was an act for which all sheriffs had a very strong dislike. This sheriff had arranged a bucket with a small hole at the bottom, which was filled with water. When a certain amount of water had dripped out, the bucket would rise very slightly, releasing the latch which opened the trap door. This saved the sheriff from actually doing the hanging. The man who was executed, by the name of Clements, lived on a very small plot of ground where he, his father and mother, and his brother and wife lived in three little separate shacks. Some of the family hadn't seen the brother nor his wife for quite some time. One day a neighbor dropped in, became suspicious, and asked where the brother and his wife had gone. He was told they just left without saying where they were going and left no forwarding address. When this was reported to the sheriff he appointed two men to go to their ranch to make further investigation. They discovered that the missing couple's clothing was still there and upon further search found some fresh dirt which had been dug up as if by coyotes. They dug further and found the two bodies, resulting ultimately in the hanging.

Adolph remembers a friend who used to tell him of his early experiences. One was about a man and his wife bringing their little baby with them across the plains. When they neared the settlement now known as Denver the mother could not nurse the baby. They stopped at a camp of friendly Indians where a squaw who had babies of her own nursed their little baby for several days. The baby's name was Jim Boutwell! He later grew up and was often mistaken for Buffalo Bill. Jim's father gave the Indians tobacco, sugar and flour for their kindness.

After Adolph's mother, Barbara died he was sent to S Bend, Ind to live with relatives; here he attended Notre Dame Acad.

Back in Denver he was employed by Daniels and Fishers Dept Store and later was a partner in establishing the American Furniture Store. He owned the Mayer Furniture Co until 1929.

Aimee attended CWC, Denver and taught cooking there. She traveled in the East, 1913-14, as a fund raiser for Natl Jewish Hosp, served as a bd mem of Childrens' Hosp Assn, 1921-55, and became an honorary member. She was active in a number of charitable organizations and in the USO during WWII. She and Adolph belonged to Temple Emanuel Synagogue.

Chn of Adolph and Aimee (Levy) Mayer

    3 i   Emily, b 13 Aug 1916
    6 ii   Adolph Jr, b 16 Feb 1919
    7 iii   Barbara, b 16 Feb 1919 twin

3 LOUIS H MAYER was born in Feb 1877 in Denver and married Minnie Kastor, adopted daughter of the Wassermans of Cheyenne, Wyo. Louis died 31 Dec 1954 and was buried in the Mayer plot at Riverside Cem. He went to Notre Dame Acad for a time and in his early business life was associated with the M D Barnett Co; later he had his own business. He was elected to the Colo Legislature in 1919. People found him a very attractive man and he was popular in social circles. When he and Minnie both became ill in 1932 he sold his business, and she went to stay with her parents who had moved to Chicago, but she never returned.

4 SAMUEL BENJAMIN MAYER was born 16 Aug 1879 in Saguache and was married at Montgomery, Ala to Irma Rice 16 Mar 1921. The daughter of Alexander and Nannette (Weil) Rice, she was born 4 Jun 1891, died 11 Dec 1958, and was buried at Fairmount as was Sam after his death 28 Feb 1964.

In Denver Samuel attended Emerson Sch and Manual Training HS. His first job after business coll was with the May Co. He owned the Star Furniture Co until the Depression in 1929 and Freeland-Mayer Chevrolet for a brief period ending in 1936. Irma attended Randolph Macon Coll and business coll. She published garden articles and children's stories as well as some verse. Sam was a bridge buff and had a remarkable sense of humor. They were members of Temple Emanuel and later Temple Micah. Although Sam was born in Saguache and loved it himself, he would never take his family there to see where and how he had lived when he was a child.

Chn of Samuel and Irma (Rice) Mayer

      i   Alex, b 12 Mar 1922 Denver; studied at Harvard; grad CU, Boulder; social worker with Protective Svcs, Denver Welfare Dept
    8 ii   Ruth, b 1 Sep 1925

5 EMILY MAYER was born in Denver 13 Aug 1916 where she was married to Leon Selig 8 Sep 1938. He was born 20 Jun 1909 in St Louis, Mo to Mortimer and Florence Selig and is self employed in real estate. He has served in many volunteer capacities such as Pres of Denver Fed of Community Ctrs, on bds of Rky Mtn and Denver Planned Parenthoods and on committees of Planned Parenthood Fed of America. Emily is also an active volunteer, serving on the bds of Santa Claus Shop, Denver Planned Parenthood, YWCA, Childrens' Hosp Aux and Human Svcs, Inc.

Chn of Leon and Emily (Mayer) Selig

    9 i   Andrew, b 10 Jun 1943
    10 ii   Mary Ellen, b 24 Sep 1947

6 ADOLPH MAYER JR was born 16 Feb 1919 in Denver. His wife, Eileen Barnett, was born there 17 Jan 1921 to Louis and Rose Barnett and they were wed 14 Sep 1943. "Bud" is Dir of Pub Relations and Communications at Denver U and is in *Who's Who in the West*, is widely active in community affairs, and has held many national public relations offices. They have two children: Reed F born 12 Mar 1945 in San Francisco, received his MA degree from Seattle U and is a juvenile rehabilitation counselor in Everett, Wash; Meredith A born 19 Nov 1951 in Denver, is a graduate of Colo U.

7 BARBARA MAYER was born 16 Feb 1919 in Denver where she became the bride of Albert Ambrose 19 Jan 1940. They are div and Barbara lives in Denver and is the proud possessor of the Family Bible.

Ch of Albert and Barbara (Mayer) Ambrose

    11 i   Claudia, b 20 June 1945

8 RUTH MAYER was born in Denver 1 Sep 1925 where she was married to (1) William Lipper 19 Dec 1948. They were div 27 Aug 1970 and Ruth married (2) Robert E Stewart in Denver 10 Jan 1975. She is a graduate of Denver U from which she received her MA in Psych and presently she is with a mail order house as a clerical worker. Robert is an insurance agt in Colo Spgs where they reside.

Chn of William and Ruth (Mayer) Lipper

    12 i   Wendy Susan, b 20 Jan 1950
      ii   Terry Lynn, b 21 Apr 1952; lives in Cal
      iii   Carol Ann, b 21 Apr 1952, twin; med student CU, Denver
      iv   Richard James, b 21 Apr 1954; lives in Cal
      v   Douglas Jonathan, b 7 Sep 1960; student CU

9 ANDREW SELIG was born in Denver 10 Jun 1943. His bride, Ellen Wise was born to Harry and Bernice (Kemler) Wise 21 Nov 1951 in Hartford, Conn and they were married 3 Jun 1973. Andrew is Chief Soc Worker at John F Kennedy Child Devel Ctr, CU Med Ctr, and family therapist and assoc prof in the Dept of Psychiatry at CU Med Sch. Their two children are Sara born 17 Jul 1976 in Vancouver, BC, Can and Rebecca Emilee 15 Jun 1979 in Denver.

10 MARY ELLEN SELIG was born 24 Sep 1947 in Denver and her husband, Robert Justice was born there 5 Feb 1947 to Ronald and Margaret Hayden. They were wed 8 Sep 1968 in Denver and their children are Aimee born 26 Jan 1972 in Tulsa, Okla and Andrea 4 Aug 1974 in Denver.

11 CLAUDIA AMBROSE, born in Denver 20 Jun 1945, was married to _____ Slater and div. She is now deceased. They had two sons, Patrick born 16 Aug 1966 and Adam Nov 1970.

12 WENDY SUSAN LIPPER was born in Denver 20 Jan 1950. Her husband is Douglas Jay Rucker whom she married there 11 Jul 1970. He was born in Ponca City, Okla 12 Apr 1948 and is a petroleum engr for Atlantic Richfield. They live in Houston, Tex with their children, Kevin James born 5 Dec 1970

216

in Anchorage, Alas, Jeffrey 15 Sep 1973 in Corpus Christi, Tex
and Paul David 15 Apr 1975 in Lafayette, Ind.

Contributors: Bud Mayer, Andrew Selig, Emily (Mayer) Selig,
Ruth (Mayer) Stewart.

My Maternal great grandmother's
Obituary Emma Uri Levi Bernheim

Services will be held this afternoon for Mrs. Emma U. Bernheim, who died Tuesday at the age of 82. The services will be held from the home, Rabbi Feinberg officiating.

Surviving are her husband, Isaac W. Bernheim, retired distillery executive; two daughters, Mrs. Adolph Mayer and Mrs. Julius Wallbrun, both of Denver; and four grandchildren, Mrs. Leon Selig of Salt Lake City, Mrs. Albert Ambrose of Denver; Adolph Mayer, Jr., and Pvt. William Wallbrun, who is now in the army.

Article about my paternal great
grandfather William Einstein

MINING ENGINEER, ON JOB DAILY, CELEBRATES 91ST BIRTHDAY

William Einstein of 5267 Washington avenue was 91 years old Thursday. Despite his age, he continues to be active in his profession of mining engineering, and goes to his office in the Security Building daily.

"A life out of doors, care in the food I eat and long daily walks," says Einstein, "are the only reasons I can give for living as long as I have."

He can read without glasses, and is in good health in every way.

Einstein was born at Offenbachen, Germany, July 27, 1831. He came to America in 1849, following the German revolts of 1848, and first settled in New York City, coming West to St. Louis in 1850. He established the first silver mine in Missouri, near Fredericktown, a few years later. He has had nine children and has outlived six of them. The three now alive are Robert Einstein, 52 years old; Mrs. Eugene L. Isaacs, 57, and Mrs. M. Selig, 41, all of St. Louis. He has eight grandchildren and three great-grandchildren, the last of whom was born a day before Einstein's ninety-first birthday, the son of his grandson, J. L. Isaacs of 6920 Pershing avenue.

WILLIAM EINSTEIN, WHO LIVED MUCH OUT-OF-DOORS, DIES AT 91

Mining Engineer, Who Took Daily Long Walks, was at Office Up to Last Saturday.

William Einstein of 5267 Washington avenue, who although he was 91 years old, had gone daily to his office in the Security Building until last Saturday, when he contracted a cold, died at 6:30 p. m. yesterday at his home of pneumonia.

Einstein, a mining engineer, celebrated his ninety-first birthday, July 27. He lived out-of-doors as much as possible and took long walks daily. He came to New York in 1849 from his birthplace in Offenbachen, Germany. The next year he came to St. Louis, and a few years later established the first Missouri silver mine, near Frederickstown.

He outlived six of his nine children. The three surviving are Mrs. Eugene L. Isaacs, with whom he resided; Mrs. M. Selig, and Robert Einstein. There are eight grandchildren and four great-grandchildren. Funeral services will be privately held tomorrow afternoon from the residence.

William Einstein, my paternal great grandfather, wrote this letter to my great aunt in 1888 and later to my grandmother. It's his advice about life and how to live in a marriage. I wish I'd followed it more regularly. The following is a typed version of the letter.

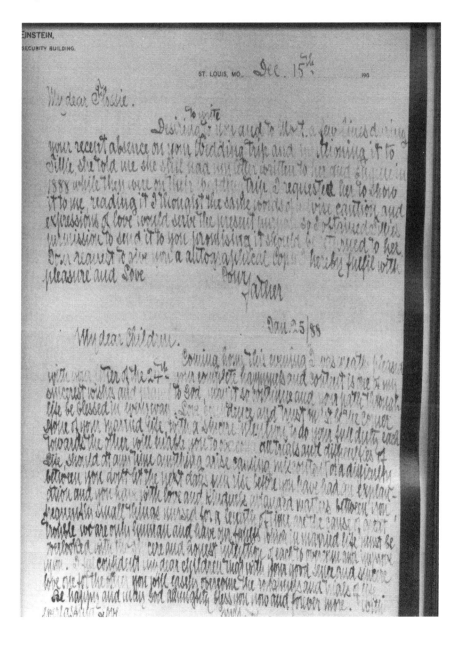

William Einstein,
       Security Building

St Louis, MO Dec. 15th 1904

My dear Flossie,

Desiring to write to you and to Mort a few lines during your recent absence on your wedding trip and mentioning it to Tillie, she told me she still had my letter written to her and Eugene in 1888 while they were on their wedding trip. I requested her to show it to me, reading it I thought the same words of advice, caution, and expressions of love would serve the present purpose so I obtained Tillie's permission to send it to you promising it should be returned to her. Your request to give you an autographical copy I hereby fulfil with pleasure and love,

Your father

My dear Children,   Jan 25/1888

Coming home this evening I was greatly pleased with your letter of the 24th Your complete happiness and content is one of my sincerest wishes and prayers to God, may it so continue your path through life be blessed in everyway. Love, confidence and trust must be the cornerstone of your married life, with a sincere intention to do your full duty each towards the other will enable you to overcome all trials and difficulties of life, should at any time anything arise causing miscontent or a difficulty between you don't let the next day's sun rise before you have had an explanation and you have with love and kindness arranged matters between you, frequently small things nursed for a length of time are the cause of great trouble. We are only human and have our faults which in married life must be overlooked with sincere and honest intention of each to overcome and improve upon. I feel confident my dear children that with your good sense and sincere love one for the other, you will easily overcome the roughness and trials of life. Be happy and may God almighty bless you now and forever more. With everlasting love

Your father

MRS. S. R. EINSTEIN'S DEATH.

Wife of Mine Promoter Passes Away Suddenly.

Mrs. Sophie Rothschild Einstein, wife of William Einstein, the mine promoter, died Tuesday evening from heart failure, at her home, No. 4009 Westminster place. Mrs. Einstein had suffered from attacks of heart trouble before, but seemed apparently in her usual health Tuesday. She was 56 years old and leaves a husband and six children.

Mrs. Einstein bade good-night to her son-in-law, J. L. Isaacs, and his wife at 10 p. m. Tuesday and retired. Fifteen minutes later she called to those in the adjoining rooms that she was suffering pain, and they summoned the family physician, Doctor E. M. Senseney. Prior to his arrival Mrs. Einstein had passed away.

Mrs. Einstein was born in Offenbach, Germany. Immediately after marrying, Mr. and Mrs. Einstein came to St. Louis, in 1853. Six children were born, all of whom are living. There were four sons, A. C. and Robert E. Einstein, who are in business in St. Louis, and James H. Einstein of New York, and Arthur O. Einstein of Chicago. The two daughters are Mrs. J. L. Isaacs and Miss Florence Einstein, both of whom reside at home.

The funeral will take place at 1 p. m. Friday, from the house to Mount Sinai Cemetery. The pallbearers will be J. D. Goldman, Fred Mayer, Meyer L. Stern, Leon Selig, E. M. Schwarzkopf, Albert Rothschild, Samuel Godlove and Moses N. Sale.

My eulogy for Gregg at his service in 2012

Gregg was the son I'd always wanted, a very special and close friend, and a valued professional colleague. The specialness and depth of these interrelated roles only grew stronger as the years went by.

I can't separate his enormous strengths and contributions to my life in each role because he demonstrated all of them in each role as a son, friend, and colleague. Others will talk or have talked about his enormous core strength, surrounded by his compassion, listening gifts, thoughtfulness, optimism, humility, tolerance and drive to bring greater cohesiveness and community to everybody whom he met. Instead, I want to share a few of the many memorable examples of our very special and uncommon relationship.

I can't imagine anybody else asking my opinion more often than Gregg did and always giving me the feeling that he valued it. Our conversations were frequent and full of depth and breadth. Not much makes an older person, and father-in-law, feel more valued than having his views and input solicited by a younger person, who is in his own right a very competent and capable person.

Our professional relationship was multi-faceted. For many months we worked together with an exciting company in New Jersey. After many long, exhilarating, and exhausting days working, we would walk for miles discussing the day, the work, what we did, how we could have done better, and often many other aspects of life.

Gregg was an expert at cutting deals. One example was his ability to somehow talk airline employees into upgrading seats when we flew on business trips. On one occasion he gave me my boarding pass before we boarded, and I had no idea what he had done until I boarded and looked at my seat. It was in first class and he told me he was unable to secure two seats in first class – Gregg being who he was, wouldn't even consider keeping it for himself.

Talking and sharing experiences, feelings, and thoughts with Gregg was always a pleasure. We would sit for hours talking on many trips to shopping malls while the women in our family shopped. We talked about our respective dreams, like our similar desire to have a mountain home at the apex of a big open valley just at the base of mountains surrounding it on three sides. We would also talk about going back to Wyoming to see the ranch he worked at when he first came west, and to once again find and be in awe of the wolves in the Lamar Valley in Yellowstone National Park.

It was so much fun looking forward to and then doing things with Gregg. I'll always remember hiking in Jackson Hole and looking forward to walking up the mountain with Gregg. However, it was obvious that I could not come close to keeping up with him, so I told him he should go on without me. This was probably the only time in our entire relationship where he did go on without me. The image of his long and fast stride making increasing distance between us is still vivid. Another shared experience that stands out in my mind is walking on the beach in Mexico when we unexpectedly came upon a nudist beach. I'm sure you can imagine what an uncomfortable and embarrassing situation this was for both of us, although I have to admit I kept trying to get him to take walks with me every day after that!

We shared a lot of common interests and values. Native American art and weaving, good bourbon, which I'd never buy for myself but Gregg bought for me, wildlife, investing, viewing people in context, the importance of taking responsibility for our actions, and understanding and helping others. I will sorely miss our many conversations together.

In the end, for me, Gregg's most important and enduring qualities were his willingness and ability to love and respect others, bring others out and give to them, and continually show tolerance and understanding, even in the most difficult of situations. Even before Gregg and Sara married, they knew what they faced, at least as much as anybody could know at that stage. In spite of the continuous horrendous challenges they continually confronted, his values and their strong characters shone through. I will continually strive to live up to Gregg's example of consistently demonstrating these values. I just wish I could reverse our roles now and be the one who solicits his opinions and input to find out how he thinks I'm doing.

Gregg took a piece of my heart with him. I will always miss him beyond comprehension and will always love and respect him for who he was and who he will continue to be for me.

Ellen's Parents.

I admired and respected Ellen's parents, although we were never close. Her father's parents were born in Russia and emigrated to America with absolutely nothing. Her father was the oldest of five and the only one who attended college. He graduated from Harvard Law School and was a lawyer all his life.

Like my dad, he was in his early thirties when he enlisted in the Navy as an officer. I bonded with him to some extent over his experiences in the military, because I was genuinely curious and interested in what he had to say about that part of his life. I got the sense that many of his experiences were traumatic. More than once, I heard him say, "What was a Jewish boy with a law degree doing in the South Pacific?"

He was stationed on the small island of Tulagi where his outfit serviced PT boats. I believe he mentioned that he'd met John F. Kennedy there. He and I shared a good laugh once when he told me about the Navy giving bras to the native women, thinking that would minimize sexual interaction between the servicemen and the island women. He told me the women had never seen such a thing, and he'd watch them walking up and down the beach carrying the bras and using the cups to gather seashells.

He never mentioned if he got close to any of the women, but he did come home with a small collection of seashells.

Later in his life, he got Alzheimer's and Parkinson's diseases. He was terrified that he would be drafted again. It was agonizing to bear witness to his fear. It must have been doubly terrifying to be the one experiencing it.

Having seen the lasting effect of war on my father-in-law, I've come to the conclusion that it became a defining moment of the lives of those who served.

Bernice, Ellen's mom, experienced several major losses early in life. Her mother died when she was five and her father when she was fifteen. Her grandmother helped care for her and her brother until she died when Bernice was sixteen, and after that their aunts took the parental role. Bernice was generous, smart, and a gifted musician. After she died, her brother told us that after high school she could have been a concert pianist. She attended Smith College and became a teacher, substitute teaching while her children were young, and then going back to school to obtain her Master of Library Science degree. She became a junior/senior high school librarian and got along well with the kids as she taught them the value of reading and learning, which were always important to her.

Sadly, I feel that we didn't really click, probably because she didn't meet my needs for attention and recognition, but I certainly had great respect for her. She also did her best to connect with me, buying my favorite onion bread and artichoke hearts when we came to visit.

Bernice also got Alzheimer's but right until she died, she was a sweet, kind person, sitting in her wheelchair in the nursing home, a gentle smile always on her face.

Erma Bombeck was a beloved syndicated columnist for many years. My mother asked a friend to send this to me when I was an adult, well past the most rascally stage of my life. Her handwritten note on the side of the column said, "Isn't this nice? Send on to Andy please."

AT WIT'S END

By Erma Bombeck

"Every family's got at least one. The child who will not conform – the rebel, the loner, the renegade, the one who is different.

"As a preschooler, he's the wiry one with the active thyroid – the one who gets locked in rest rooms because he stayed behind to find out where the water went when you pushed down the handle. He's the one who wanders away from home and gets his arm stuck in a piece of construction pipe. He's the one who rejects store-bought toy in favor of taking the registers out and making tunnels out of old oatmeal boxes. He gets more lickings than all the other kids put together.

"In school, gets checkmarks for daydreaming, for not being neat, for not working to capacity. It doesn't seem to bother him. In his preoccupation with other things, he is unaware that he drives his family crazy, arriving late for dinner every night, wearing his socks and underwear to bed to save time in the mornings, cutting the grass only when he needs the money.

"The older he gets, the less aware he becomes of his odds with the world. There aren't enough weekends for his interests and his projects. In the garage is his 'pumping heart,' which he devised out of plastic sandwich bags, tubing and cake coloring. Cluttering the bedroom all the remains of his puppet show with the blanket (curtain) tucked in the top bunk bed. On the table is his latest book (It takes an entire afternoon to write them.), entitled, 'Floyd, The Story of an Insecure Snake With Bad Breath.'

"Parents are awed by genius. They are content with an average child. They are compassionate toward the slow learner. But the child who stands apart and is none of these only puzzles, confuses, and tires their patience.

"They confess to each other their fears for his future, this child who is unpredictable and not only out-of-step with the world but whose feet rarely touch the ground. 'What's to become of him?'

"Some of these children with their insatiable curiosity and hard-headed drive, will beat paths of greatness and discovery, the likes of Winston Churchill, perhaps.

"Others won't be great at all, but with their enthusiasm, imagination, creativity and penchant for living life to the fullest, who is to say they are not the first to touch the stars?

"So he is accident-prone because he daydreams, he gets bit by animals because he's foolishly trusting, maintains a closet that the insurance company refuses to insure. Look at him closely. He's something special to remind us all that life is precious gift to be lived to its fullest.

"And as Henry David Thoreau said, 'If a man does not keep pace with his companions, perhaps it is because he hears a different drummer. Let him step to the music which he hears.'"

-1966 Newsday Inc.

Made in the USA
Monee, IL
05 April 2025

5d31b0e2-169b-4ba7-afea-79ccd8f496b3R01